Davinia Tomlinson • Andrea Oerter

Frances Lincoln
Children's Books

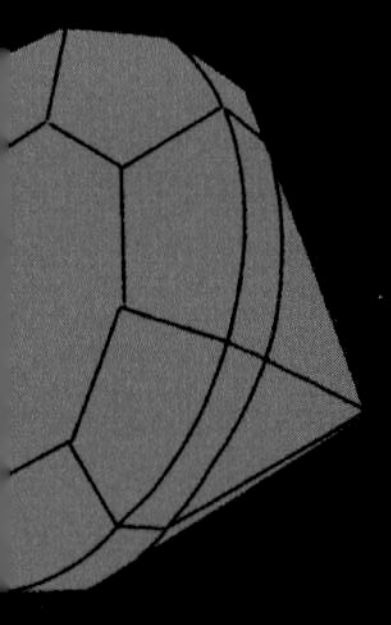

Contents

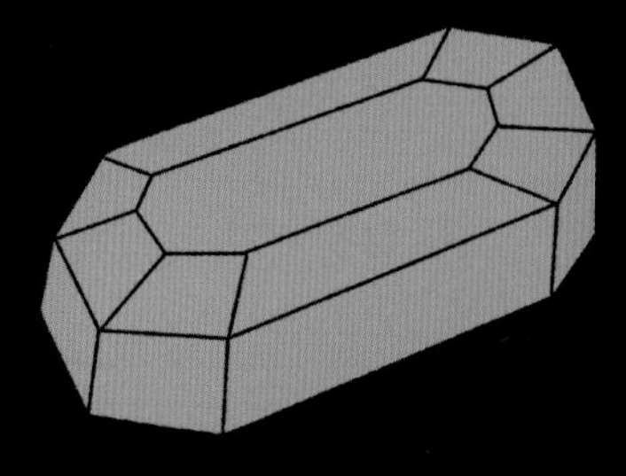

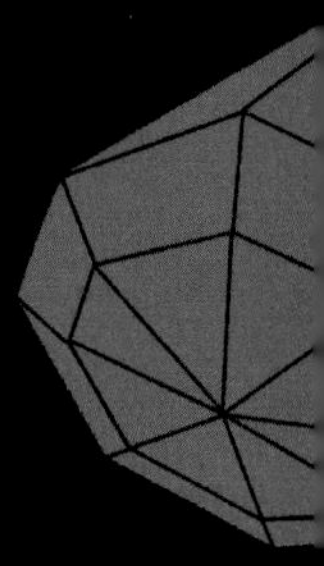

Hi there,

If you're reading this, then chances are you've got more than a passing interest in how to manage your money effectively. If not, then maybe somebody gave you this book, which means that the people in your life love you enough to want to make sure you're ready to enter adulthood, with everything you need to succeed. The good news is whichever of these camps you fall into, you're in the right place. The even better news is that the lessons in this book, if applied consistently, will set you up to adopt good money habits for the rest of your life. No, seriously.

I'm Davinia and I spend most of my days thinking about how to get more money in the hands of more women. Not because I'm money-obsessed (when has that ever worked out well for anyone?) but because the reality is, we could do with a little help in this area. You may be surprised to discover that, despite the female population excelling in lots of ways overall, from academic life to our chosen careers, women all over the world face significant challenges when it comes to cash.

We earn less, we invest less, and we struggle more financially when we reach old age. This is not OK.

But we're going to do something about it. Starting with this book.

You, dear reader, have the potential to do great things (I'm sure you've probably already started) and one of the best ways to unleash that potential is through knowledge. By the end of this book, I want you to feel ready to take on the world, and to contribute to it in a way that is more equitable and financially fair for all. My job is to help guide you along the way.

Just think of me as your financial fairy godmother, with all the wisdom and the sparkle but without the magic spells. Couldn't stretch to that unfortunately.

Love,

Dav x

CHAPTER ONE

WHY W€ NE£D TO $TART TALKING ABOUT MONE¥

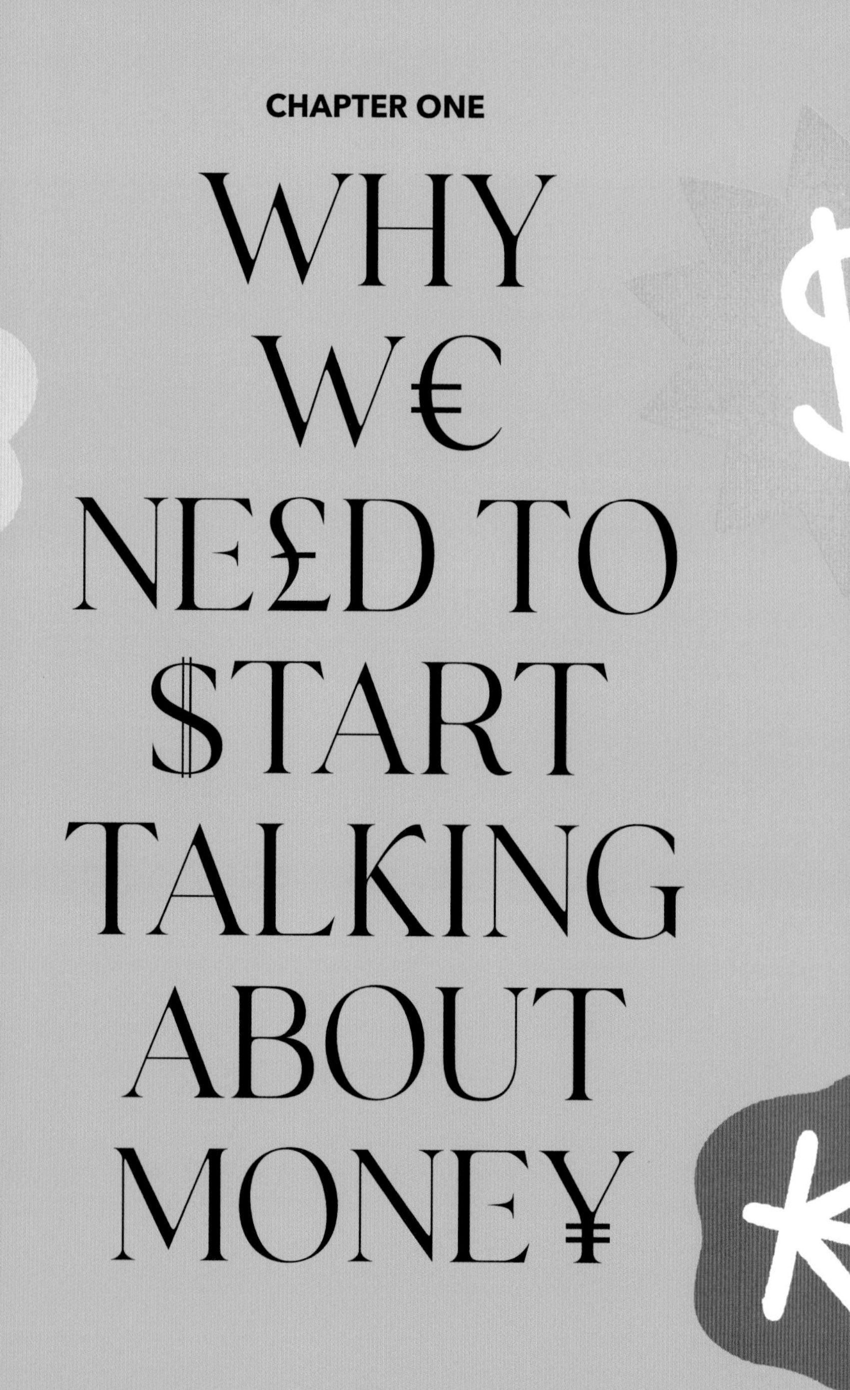

When last did you think about your money?

I mean **really** think about it. Beyond your day-to day-spending and the occasional daydream, which may or may not include things like:

1) How much money you have;
2) How much money you wish you had; and
3) What you intend to do with your money once you've closed the gap between points 1 and 2!

No, when did you think more deeply about your cash? The above are all important, don't get me wrong. And spoiler alert: these will probably still be your top three considerations as you get older too.

But I'd be willing to bet (money of course), that the idea of looking a bit closer at your cash and considering not just what you have today, but also how to build upon it to do amazing things in the future, is probably not something you've spent a whole lot of time thinking about.

And if not, I hear you. Anything finance- or money-related has got a bit of an image problem to be honest. A makeover is long overdue. But guess what? Now is quite possibly the absolute best time to be thinking about your finances.

Why? Well, you might be surprised to hear this, but there are millions of adults all over the world whose first introduction to managing their money was when they got their first jobs.

Yes, there are the exceptions who start earning their own money sooner. Maybe you babysit your neighbors' kids a few hours a week, build websites, walk dogs, or sell stuff to your other friends. In which case you're already off to a flying start.

But for lots of us, the first time we ever earn a proper paycheck is in our twenties. By which point, there are probably so many habits we've picked up from watching others manage their money, some good some not so good, as well as all the potential pitfalls we may encounter along the way, that our chances of making savvy money moves from day one are already likely to be reduced.

If you think about it of course this makes perfect sense. How could you possibly be good at doing something if you've never been taught how? Or at the very least had someone nurture your natural born talents to be even greater?

Imagine some of your favorite hobbies. Gaming, dancing, athletics, coding, music classes —whatever it is you enjoy. This hobby probably started to feel really good the more experienced you became at it. Nobody likes being annihilated in their favorite computer game time after time. So you practice and study, you refine and review until you get so good that you can beat your opponents without even breaking a sweat.

The same principle applies to money.

Waiting until you have money to learn what to do with money makes no sense.

Just as you wouldn't expect Naomi Osaka or Serena Williams to have achieved their sporting success without years of coaching and study beforehand, you can't expect to get *good with money* without learning the basics first.

Girls and Money

But let's get the elephant out the room first shall we? You know, the giant pink one that we're all too afraid to mention for fear of causing offense? Yeah, that elephant.

You may be wondering why this book is all about girls. After all, money isn't gendered so why should books about it be? And if you were already thinking that, then I love your inquisitive mind. Don't lose that, it will take you far.

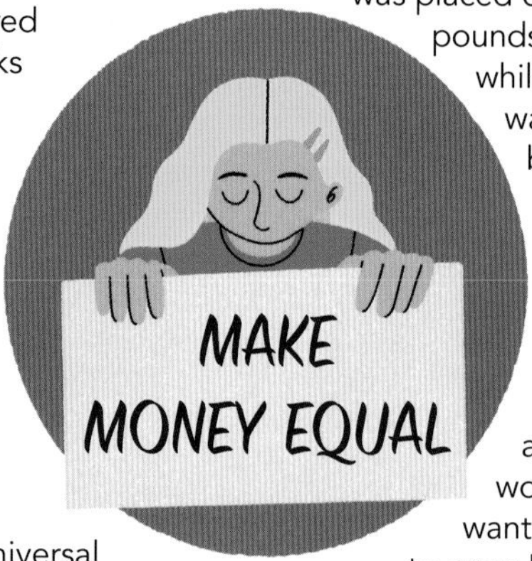

MAKE MONEY EQUAL

But let's not beat around the bush here: while money, just like love, is a universal language, it seems that the world is yet to catch up to this obvious truth. Don't believe me? Let's look at some of the evidence. One of the best ways to illustrate this point is to look at the difference between how men and women are spoken to about money.

In a brilliant piece of research called "Make Money Equal," commissioned by Starling Bank in the UK, there were some striking differences.

While advertising, press, and other media such as magazines aimed at women tended to focus on discounts, budgeting, and shaving money off our grocery bills, the same media aimed at men tended to focus on some of the more exciting elements of money management instead, such as stock-market investing or buying and selling houses for profit.

The difference in the language used was slightly suspect too—for women greater emphasis was placed on saving a few pounds here and there, while for men it was more about building wealth. But surely men want to bag a grocery bargain too (everybody eats after all!) and what woman doesn't want to know how to grow her hard-earned cash?

The quite obvious shade? That women either aren't or shouldn't be interested in anything more than the most basic money management and should really just stay in their lane.

The problem with this isn't just that it reinforces old lingering gender stereotypes that undermine **both** men and women. The fact is that there is a more fundamental issue at stake too.

THE GOOD NEWS

Overall, women are living well into old age all over the world, giving us a longer time to enjoy life after we stop working.

THE NOT SO GOOD NEWS

For a variety of reasons, we're generally saving less than men for retirement, despite living longer, which means that when we do stop working, our ability to live our very best lives could be severely hampered. So how exactly will we finance those fun holidays we plan on taking with our friends?

So, when we unapologetically state **"CASH IS QUEEN"** in this book, it's not to be exclusive. It's because our long-term quality of life and, to be even more precise, our very existence depends on it.

Mind over (money) matter

Before we begin, though, we need to do a little mental housekeeping first. Because lots of the sticky situations we find ourselves in are as much about how much we know about a particular subject as they are about how much we believe we know about a particular subject.

Stick with me here, this bit is really important. Have you ever heard the expression:

"Mind over matter"
or
"It all starts in the mind"

The essence of this, of course, is that when it comes to achieving anything at all, a big chunk of it is linked to what we tell ourselves about our likelihood of success. Some of our favorite celebrities are good examples of this.

Let's take Beyoncé, for example. Whether you're a fan or not, her artistic credentials and career spanning decades, starting in childhood, can't really be questioned.

But to have achieved her level of success, she's had to be both mentally and physically prepared. She has to train really hard regularly to maintain a certain level of fitness, learn a gazillion routines for every show and confidently sing and dance at speed while tossing her head around without running out of breath.

But before she even got to the gravity-defying stage shows attracting hundreds of thousands of fans, there were the rejections and the criticism from people who did not see what she saw and who did not believe what she believed about her own potential.

And so she learned very early on that being the best wasn't just about having the greatest voice or the catchiest tunes (although that part helps hugely), but also about being very careful about what she chooses to believe about herself and who she chooses to surround herself with (we'll talk more about this later).

The point is, when we think about our overall fitness, including financial fitness, our bodies are only part of the puzzle. One of the muscles that needs exercising as much as all of the others is our minds. And whether you're Beyoncé or not, one thing is clear: if you are short on self-confidence and belief in yourself, then not only are you depriving the world of the magic we so desperately need right now, a magic that is uniquely yours, but you are also massively limiting your chances of long-term success, financial or otherwise.

I'M HERE TO MAKE SURE THAT DOESN'T HAPPEN.

The Stories We Tell Ourselves

A while ago I stumbled across this quote that really made me think:

WHETHER YOU THINK YOU CAN OR THINK YOU CAN'T –YOU'RE RIGHT.

(Henry Ford)

What a mic drop. I'm yet to come up with a better expression to convey the power of self belief.

Now, let's run through some of the stories we might be telling ourselves about our mastery of money. Here are some examples:

Let's take a look at each one in reverse order:

I don't do numbers, I'm more of a [insert stereotypically "girlie" trait here] person

Who on Earth came up with this idea? I'm not suggesting everyone should love math—we all have different talents and interests after all. But how is it possible to just opt out of a competence that applies to, well [unscientific estimate loading] 97% of our entire lives?

If this applies to you, I see you and it's OK. But this needs to change.

Knowing your numbers when it comes to looking at your money is a real boss move. And guess what? You probably already know them. You could probably tell me the last time you decided to spend or save your cash, for example, and you make decisions like these every day.

Because personal finance is less about algebra and trigonometry, and more about how to manage the money you do have to help you fulfil your wildest dreams (or, at least, pay for your lunch at school).

And that's something we can all get excited about.

I'm just no good with money, as soon as I get it, it goes!

This goes back to that quote by Henry Ford—what do you think is the impact of your brain receiving this message over and over again?

Let's put it like this: if your brain informs your thoughts and your thoughts inform your actions, then it stands to reason that after a while of telling yourself you are useless with money, your actions will start to play along. Whether or not this is actually true.

Instead, why not start to rewrite this story. Change the narrative in your head to become something like:

I need to keep better track of my money so I know how I'm spending it and where.

See? A simple switch that takes the sting out of those negative words and is a welcome reminder to rethink your approach in future.

Words have power. Use yours wisely.

I usually leave anything to do with money to my dad/brother/(male) partner

It's probably a bit too soon yet to be talking about money conversations with a potential partner, but that doesn't mean there aren't other relationships you're growing up around that aren't painting a picture in your mind about who should take the lead on money discussions in your life in the future.

Who do you see taking the lead on money matters at home?

Do the opinions of male relatives carry the most weight and/or do they typically make the final decision?

Are you or other women in your life the butt of frequent jokes about how you manage your money, whether they're based on fact or fiction?

If you answered yes to any of these questions, it doesn't automatically mean that this is bad. Getting opinions from people you trust when you're making a decision is a great way to evaluate your options when you're unsure about something.

But if you find that they become your permanent go-to people at the expense of some of the women in your life, specifically when there's a money matter to be discussed, or that it's become normal to trash-talk your financial knowledge, then it might be worth asking yourself why you still refer to them.

Now for some science – the money scripts

In 2011, father and son psychologists Brad and Ted Klontz came up with a brilliant way to describe some of the beliefs we hold about money and where they come from. According to them, our money scripts are unconscious beliefs we hold about money that are typically rooted in childhood.

These beliefs are described as "unconscious" because, although we are not aware of them happening at the time, we absorb them daily and they massively influence how we live our lives. Just like the air that we breathe.

Imagine some of the things you pick up from the people in your household every day just by listening and observing. Things like:

- Jogging every day is a good way to relieve stress and we know this because dad comes back in a much better mood after a run; or

- Not speaking negatively about others is a great way to achieve inner peace and we know this because mom always shuts down any gossip from the neighbors and as a result has great relationships with the people on your street.

Our money scripts are no different. They influence not just how we behave with money but the financial outcomes we achieve as adults too. In their study, Brad and Ted Klontz identified four different personalities associated with our relationship with money.

1) MONEY STATUS

Meet Monique

"I always feel so much better about myself the more money I have. It's such a downer being broke and really affects my mood.

We didn't have a lot of money growing up so I'm making up for lost time. I love designer clothes and gadgets, which cost a fortune but no sweat, if I can't afford them I'll just stick it on my credit card. I'll pay it off eventually but there's no rush. Image is so important so I can't be caught slipping—especially not on the 'gram!

My mom and dad still give me an allowance even though I live by myself but I need this to make sure I can still buy the things I like. I haven't told my boyfriend about this though, so sshhhh!"

2) MONEY WORSHIP

Meet Parker

"You know that saying money doesn't buy happiness? Well I don't know who came up with it because it's totally wrong. Money absolutely buys happiness. At least it does for me. I literally have no idea how anybody could be happy without it. The trouble is the more money I get, the more I want so I don't know if I'll ever achieve true happiness but it's a risk I'm willing to take!

I'm a bit obsessive about the things I love, whether it's basketball that I played at college, my pet kitten Mimi or money, and will put them before everything else including my family. I won't stop until I get what I want and earn the kind of money that will help me live the life of my wildest dreams."

3) MONEY VIGILANT

Meet Tolu

"I'm an avid saver and have been from the day I got my very first piggy bank when I was six. My grandma was a successful businesswoman and had a huge influence on me growing up. I spent all my weekends with her and used to watch her budgeting, balancing the books, and running the household finances too. She would always tell me to live below my means and to only spend exactly what I could afford and not a penny more. She grew up in a household where there wasn't a lot of money around so she's super resourceful and always reminds me that a young woman needs to have her own money and be able to manage it wisely so that's what I try to do.

I was lucky enough to have my parents pay for college but I had a part-time job while studying to pay for everything else. I actually graduated with savings! I don't like to depend on others for things I want or need. I don't need that much anyway. I rarely go out, buy my clothes secondhand or sew them myself and have had the same cell phone for about eight years. I'm going to see how long I can make it last for!

My friends say I worry too much about money and need to learn to let my hair down but I never want to be in a situation where I struggle financially now or in the future so I'll stick with my approach!"

4) MONEY AVOIDANCE

Meet Layla

"Both my parents are medics and encouraged me and my brother to take that route too. They want the best for us and so it made sense to them. I enjoy being a doctor and love helping people but it seems perverse to be paid so much for doing so. I've moved up the ladder really quickly for someone of my age which is good I suppose, but I find the amount of money I earn really cringey, especially when I compare it to some of my friends who are struggling to make ends meet. As a result I'm constantly lending them money and never expect them to pay it back.

I haven't got a clue what's in my bank account. I spend without bothering to check. I'm fairly confident that I'm not in my overdraft, but that's about it.

From what I can gather, no good ever comes from a fixation with money and I've never met anyone earning huge amounts that I've liked so I just avoid the subject completely."

ACTIVITY

Which one of these personalities is most like you? Do any of these sound familiar? This is a great conversation to start with the adults in your life, whether that's parents, aunties, or teachers. Discuss this with the grown-ups at home and see whether there are any surprises.

AFFIRMATIONS FOR A ROYAL MONEY MINDSET (RMM)

Now that we can see where some of the beliefs we might hold about our ability to make money magic may come from, let's close the chapter by having a go at rewriting these scripts and stories to paint a more positive picture.

Here are some affirmations or mantras to repeat to yourself as a reminder to help you maintain a positive outlook:

1) I deserve to enjoy the money I work so hard for and use it to pay for experiences that bring me happiness.

2) I am good, if not great, with numbers—I make micro calculations that improve my life, every single day.

3) I control my money, my money doesn't control me.

4) My worth is not tied to how much money I make. I am valuable and worthy just as I am.

ACTIVITY

Grab another piece of paper or continue in your notebook and think carefully about how you might answer the below:

My personal wealth is about more than just money.

The other things that help me live a happy life include...

You can write as many examples as you want and they can be as varied as you like. Here's my answer:

My personal wealth is about more than just money. The other things that help me live a happy life include spending time in the sunshine, strawberry ice-cream, my two daughters, learning new languages and cultures, and discovering new fruits from around the world: current favorite—rambutan!

How about you?

About this book

At some point in your life, you may hear the expression "cash is king." Typically used in business, to signal the importance of keeping a healthy flow of cash both into and out of the business.

But remember that money makeover I told you about?

Well that's going to have to start with us.

Because in this book not only is cash queen, we are too.

Especially when it comes to making positive choices for ourselves and influencing the people around us to make smart choices too.

But what does it really take to become a true money queen? Or in other words, to develop a Royal Money Mindset? Let's start by coming up with some words that immediately spring to mind when we hear the word "royalty":

• Leadership—of ourselves and others.

• Pride—in who we are and what we stand for.

• Luxury—unapologetically enjoying the things that spark joy.

• Self-respect—treating ourselves with care.

• Integrity—being clear on our values and acting accordingly
The same could easily apply to our money.

Our Royal Money Mindset is not just about how we manage ourselves, but how we impact others too. It's about trusting in our money-management ability and speaking positively about what we can achieve. By the end of the book, this will become second nature.

Throughout the following chapters we'll cover the top ten money lessons you should know by the time you're eighteen. There are lots more that you will learn over the course of your life but the ones you will read in this book, tried and tested over years, will act as a springboard for whatever you go on to do next.

Young women just like you ask me all the time for my advice on some of their money conundrums and it's always a real joy to play agony aunt! Some of the most common questions I get asked are also shared here with my top tips on how to overcome them because the likelihood is they'll help you too.

Oh and to help you stay on track, there will be a couple of quick reflections within each chapter to help you remember the main points and keep on course (just like the ones above). We'll call these **"Crown Jewels."**

By the time you finish reading this book you will know:

• The essential ingredients in the mix to help you build solid financial foundations beneath everything you do.

• Why living within your means doesn't have to be at odds with living your best life.

• How to set financial goals that you can stick to and achieve.

• Why learning how to take care of your money at an early age is one of the most BOSS moves you can make.

You ready? Let's go.

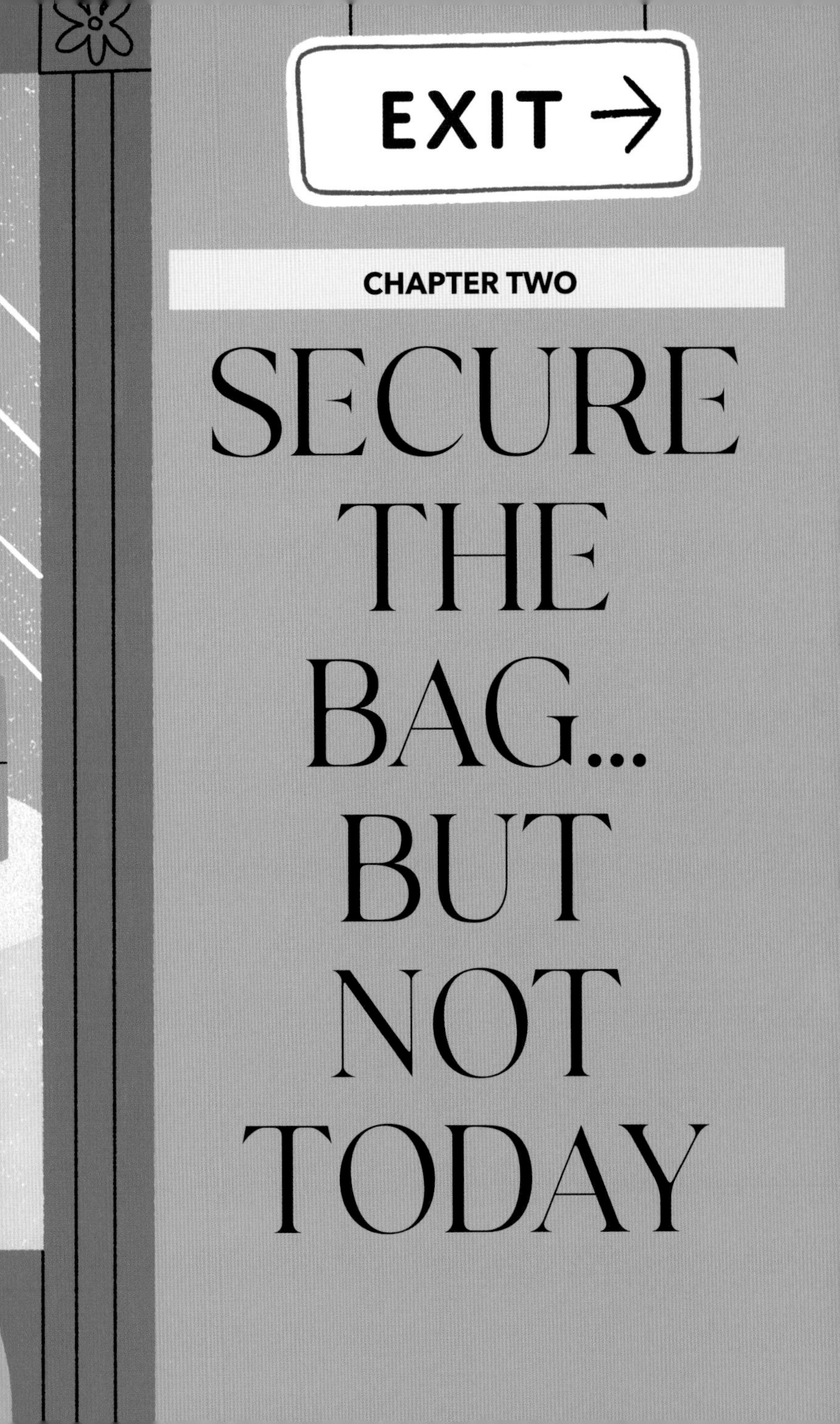

CHAPTER TWO

SECURE THE BAG... BUT NOT TODAY

Let's start at the start. What do we mean by gratification?

You've probably been learning about the concept of gratification from the day you were born, without you even realizing it.

Most of us, myself included, will have had this drummed into us by parents, carers, aunts, and uncles as one of life's great lessons. However, it's unlikely to have been presented to you with a drum roll every time someone advised you to do something, however entertaining that thought might be. Although it might make things easier in some cases, if all of "LIFE'S GREAT LESSONS" were presented to you in flashing neon with an arrow pointing towards them, in the absence of that, let's start by taking a look at the dictionary definition of gratification:

"A state of being pleased or satisfied with the fulfilment of a desire."

Or, in other words, that feel-good factor you get from obtaining something you really, really want.

But did you know that there are two different types of gratification? They're called "immediate" and "deferred."

In this chapter, we'll explore them both, breaking down how they might work in real life and explaining why mastering this principle is key to cultivating your Royal Money Mindset.

Immediate vs deferred gratification

Have you ever saved up for something you really wanted, diligently stashing your money away week after week, month after month?

How good did it feel when you eventually got it in your hands? Amazing right? That's deferred, or delayed gratification. The idea that by making sacrifices now, you will put yourself in line for a greater reward in future.

On the other hand, immediate gratification relates to satisfying an instant desire for something, deciding that, on balance, you'd rather have it now than to wait. Which of these types of gratification do you think is best? If you answered, "it depends," then you'd be right. There's a time and a place for both and knowing when to switch between the two is your secret weapon.

But when it comes to achieving your goals, there are some pretty compelling reasons why we all need to learn the gift of patience.

To understand these better, let's take a look at the science.

The Marshmallow Experiment

A few decades ago, possibly before some of your parents were born, a psychologist called Walter Mischel at Stanford University, in sunny California, did an experiment designed exclusively to understand human behavior around gratification. It was called the Marshmallow Experiment.

He selected a group of four-year-olds, gave them each a yummy marshmallow treat and allowed them to choose one of two options:

a) They could either eat the treat straightaway; or

b) Wait a short time after which they would receive two treats.

Any marshmallow fans out there? Which option would you choose?

As you might expect, lots of the children ate their marshmallow straightaway. The temptation was simply too great for them to resist. And who could blame them? With no previous knowledge of the research team behind the experiment, how could they possibly trust that the researchers would actually keep their promise to give them two in the future?

But some of the children were able to resist the urge to eat theirs as soon as the researchers left the room and instead decided to wait for what they hoped would be the more attractive, more substantial reward of getting two in the future.

So what might have caused the difference in behavior?

In reality, there are potentially dozens of factors which could cause this. After all, we're not robots. Even just getting up on the wrong side of bed one day might make you do or say something completely out of character. But some of the suggestions made for the original study include:

- Lack of trust: if someone gave you a treat unexpectedly but you didn't really know them that well and they'd had no track record of having done so in the past, of course you'd be suspicious. (I mean there's a broader point here about not accepting things from strangers in the first place, but let's stay focused!)

- Lack of willpower: even at that very early stage, some of the children were able to wait it out while others responded as you would expect a four-year-old to! But when it comes to making snap judgments about what to do for the best, especially when it comes to money, willpower is not to be overlooked.

- Lack of discipline: you might be thinking, well what's the difference between this and willpower? Think of willpower as something you reach for in the moment, and discipline as something that requires longer-term nerves of steel. Both essential ingredients in establishing your Royal Money Mindset.

Have a think about how you measure up against the last two points. How would you rate your willpower and discipline?

ACTIVITY

Why not try running your own experiment? Ask some of your friends if they would like to help you trial this experiment. Follow the steps below:

1) Assemble a small group of your friends.

2) Place a small treat in front of them—it doesn't need to be a marshmallow but just a treat that you know they'll love. (Always check for allergies or possibility of choking before starting.)

3) Tell them they have two options. The first option is to eat it now and just have one treat. Or the second option is to wait a few minutes after which they'll get two yummy treats.

4) Leave the room and watch them from behind the door to see what happens next!

What happened next?
Did anyone surprise you?

Why this matters

Let's go back to the marshmallows for a moment. Why would it even matter in the first place whether you ate yours in seconds or deferred it for the future. They all get eaten in the end right? Well, technically yes. But there are actually some surprising benefits to waiting.

Take the participants in the Marshmallow Experiment. In follow up studies, the researchers found that those children who could delay gratification (aka eat the marshmallow a bit later) had the edge over those children who gulped it up immediately. They had better life outcomes in a number of areas:

1) They performed better academically years later.
2) They tended to have better overall health.
3) They had much higher test scores.

What's all this got to do with money?

Quite a lot as it happens.

Your Royal Money Mindset isn't developed in a day and neither is your ability to achieve any major goal, especially financial ones. Just think of some of the plans you have for when you get a bit older.
You might want to...

Start a business.

Travel the world.

Buy your first car.

None of these goals can be achieved overnight. They require not just hard work and dedication, whether it be through study or saving, but a clear vision of where you are and where you're going to next.

But that's not to say that all goals should be far into the future. Not at all. In fact, one of the joys of life is the thrill that comes from unexpected fun. Something that you do spontaneously.

And then there are some of the other goals. You might want to...

Go to the movies with your friends.

Buy a new nail polish "just because."

Get an outfit for your bestie's birthday party.

These should not be viewed as any less valuable because you want to fulfil them quickly, quite the contrary. Neither should you feel that every possible desire or "want" should be preplanned down to the last detail.

But what does matter is that you get the balance right.

Having a clear understanding of the difference between needs and wants is a useful place to start here.

Needs vs wants

Quite simply, our needs must be fulfilled in order for us to survive. Air, shelter, food, water, and love. These are a handful of essential ingredients for us to live on a basic level.

Our wants are more like "nice to haves." Those things that we may well have our hearts set on, but which, if we're honest with ourselves, are not life or death.

ACTIVITY

- Pull out your notebook again or get some paper and spend the next five minutes going through your current list of wants. How would you categorize them?

- Is the balance right? Again, there are no hard and fast rules on this but if it's helpful, you probably want a ratio of something like 3:1 in favor of deferred gratification.

- Now spend another five minutes just reflecting on why you want them. Score your answers on a scale of 1–5 where 1 is "not clear on why you want it at all" and 5 is "the vision is so clear it's blinding!"

For anything that's a 1 or 2 try to retrace your steps to figure out why they made the list in the first place. Or, if you're feeling ruthlessly royal today, put them in the trash immediately!

DID YOU SMILE TODAY?

Golden rules of gratification

As a general rule of thumb, the best way to bring this principle to life is to follow these golden rules.

1.

BE INTENTIONAL ABOUT SAVING A PERCENTAGE OF EVERY PAYCHECK OR MONETARY GIFT YOU RECEIVE.

You may be motivated enough to save the whole thing which is great news. That kind of discipline will take you far. But try not to forego fun entirely. As you've probably already gathered, treating yourself occasionally is no bad thing. As a minimum if you always remember to save some and spend some, you'll be off to a great start. Not sure how much to put in each category? Start with a 50/50 split.

2.

UNDERSTAND YOUR OWN MOTIVATIONS FOR DECIDING WHAT TO SPEND ON.

Why do you want to buy that item or experience? I know this sounds eye-roll inducing and I can already hear you saying, "er… of course, I know why I want it, Dav." But do you really? Saying, "I want it because I want it," like my daughters do sometimes, is a hint that you might need to do a little more work here! But understanding who or what we are influenced by is a real boss move and is what will set you apart from most people, whatever their age.

Because guess what?

We are ***all*** influenced and anyone who says they're not is likely to be fibbing. The secret to your success is making sure that your influences are positive, uplifting, and, crucially, aligned to a goal or feeling you are targeting.

Not *everything* you do has to be based on a "need" otherwise we'd buy nothing other than food and water. Neither does it have to be something you only benefit from in the future. But it does need to be something you can say *with your heart* that you absolutely and unashamedly want and why.

3.

BE CLEAR ON THE URGENCY ATTACHED TO EACH DESIRE.

So now, having established your big why, you need to decide how soon you want to bring your goal to life. This is perhaps the hardest part of the process because it requires you to predict or forecast what fulfilling your current "wants" will have on your future sense of happiness and wellbeing. Not just in the instant you make your purchase, but long afterwards. And unless you're a clairvoyant, few of us can say with 100% certainty how we're going to feel. But it is important.

Why?

Because the whole point about gratification is that it is underlined by a drive to feel good. And of course one of the great secrets to life (cue that drum roll we talked about at the beginning) is how we can crank up the feel-good factor while doing no harm to one another, ourselves and the planet (well that's one of my big secrets anyway!) and to maintain the feeling as long as we possibly can. To unlock this, we have to be clear on how permanent or sustainable the feeling we are targeting will last. Otherwise we end up with a series of sugar highs that feel good at the time but which disappear virtually instantly, leading us to seek more. End result? A sickly feeling and cavities.

Not a good look.

HERE'S A RECAP

IMMEDIATE	DEFERRED
Means you're focused on what's happening right now.	Means you're focused on the future. Even if it's just the next day.
Fulfils immediate need or want.	Fulfils future need or want.
Accepts potential loss of future reward.	Accepts delay in immediate reward for chance of greater future reward.

TEST YOUR UNDERSTANDING

1) Your grandma gives you some money for your birthday. You are thrilled and decide to spend it on a new game. When you get to the store you see that you are $20 short. You hadn't realized it was so expensive. You spot another game that is the exact same amount as the money you received. You like it but it's not the one you had your heart set on. You know that you'll be paid for babysitting your neighbor's kids in the next few weeks so decide to wait until then to make up the shortfall and buy the game you really want. This is an example of:

A. Deferred gratification   B. Immediate gratification   C. Not sure

2) As you are leaving the store to make your way home, you realize that it's lunchtime and you are getting hungry. You know there's food at home so although you'd rather wait to eat your dad's delicious vegetable lasagne, you can't resist a bubble tea so decide to spend some of your money on a drink for the journey home. Yes, it will leave a small hole in the money you're saving for your game, but the happiness those little bubbles bring you when they pop in your mouth is totally worth it. Is this an example of:

A. Deferred gratification   B. Immediate gratification   C. Both

3) You get home and discover that your brother's eaten all the lasagne. He looks particularly smug about this but you resist the urge to trip him up on his way to the living room. Your mom offers to whip you up something, but her suggested options will all take at least 15 minutes. You thank her and eat a bowl of cereal instead. Delicious and quick! What is this an example of:

A. Deferred gratification   B. Immediate gratification   C. Not sure

CROWN JEWELS

So now you know how essential understanding the different forms of gratification are, here are five key things to remember.

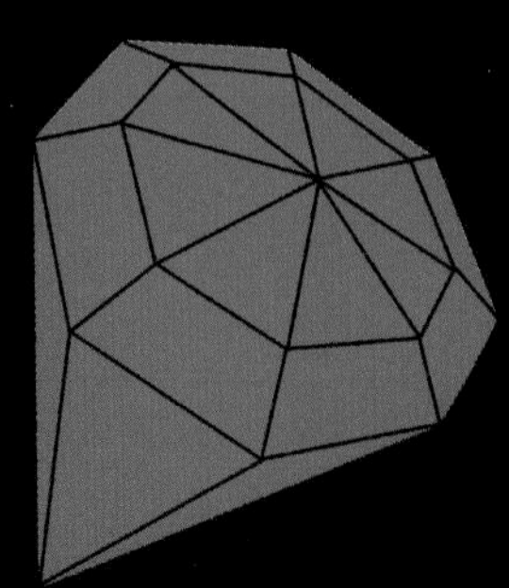

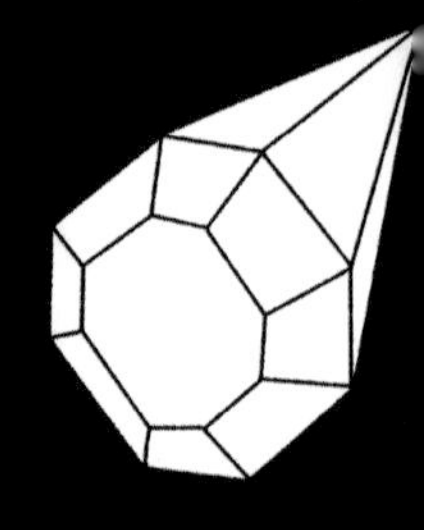

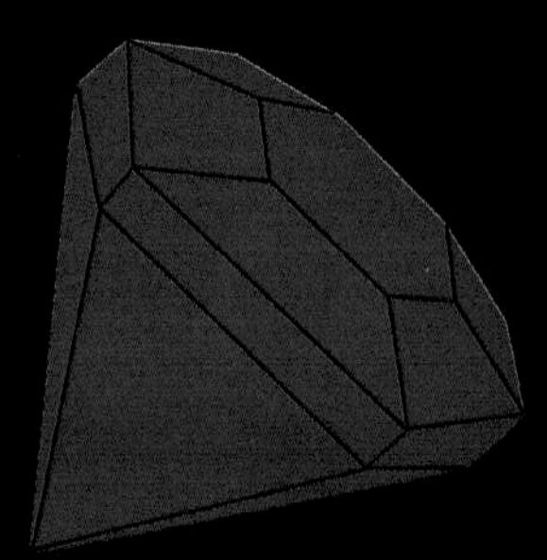

1.

Immediate gratification involves the instant fulfilment of a want or desire.

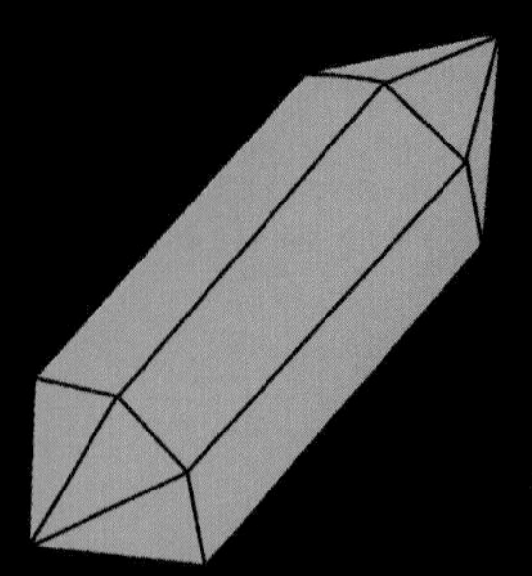

2.

Deferred gratification involves delaying satisfaction at some point in future.

3.

The Marshmallow Experiment showed that those children who were able to wait before eating their treat were more likely to have higher rates of health and academic performance over time.

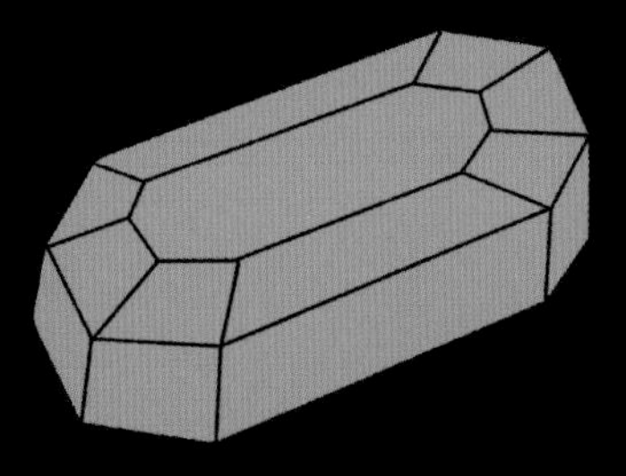

4.

Understanding the difference between your needs and wants is crucial to making the decision about which ones need to be fulfilled and when.

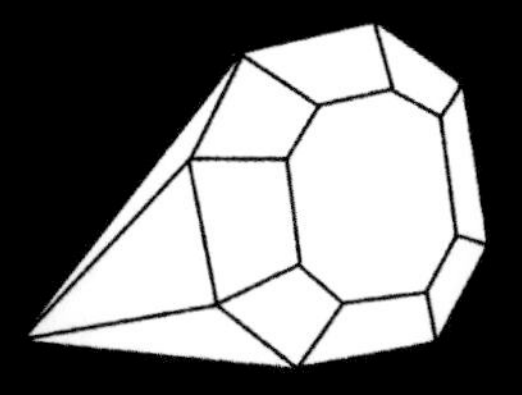

5.

There is a time and a place for both forms of gratification. One is not automatically superior to the other.

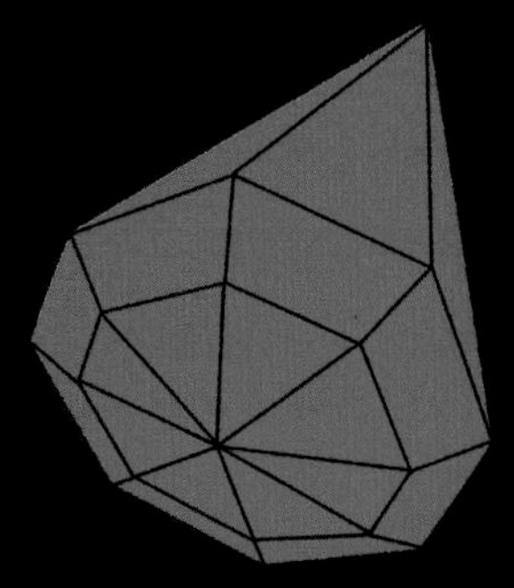

CHAPTER THREE

IT'S NOT HOW MUCH YOU MAKE,

BUT
HOW
MUCH
YOU
KEEP
THAT
COUNTS

Forget everything you've been told about how the rich and famous became that way. Well, at least part of what you've been told. You know what the unglamorous, yet practical truth is?

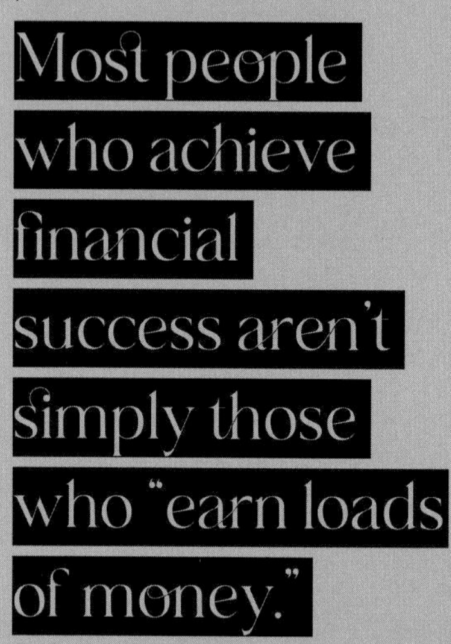

Though that is, of course, part of the story for some. In fact, the far less talked about reality is that learning how to protect your cash and guard it like a hawk, is one of the most powerful money lessons there is.

Let's say you win the lottery. Up until that point you've been fairly financially irresponsible. You spend your money on what you want, when you want, and rarely check your account. You spend more than you make and then make up the shortfall from borrowing money from others, whether it's the bank or your loved ones.

Money to you is a bit of a mystery and as quickly as it comes into your account it leaks out, seemingly at random. You find yourself scratching your head and wondering how on Earth you end up in this situation so frequently. Then suddenly you hit the jackpot.

Your bank balance goes from -10¢ to +$1m quite literally overnight. Can you imagine it?

It's quite a surreal thought for lots of us. You're over the moon and excitedly make plans for your newfound riches.

Buy your sister a house.

Buy your brother a car.

Pay off your parents' mortgage.

And that's before we even get to your list!

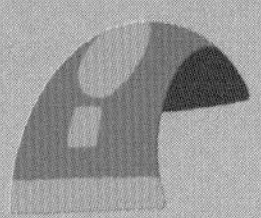

ACTIVITY

Now imagine that you've received a big amount of cash unexpectedly. What would you do with all the money? Pull out that notebook once more, or grab a piece of paper, and write down some ideas that pop into your head. Maybe aim for five to begin with but if you can think of more then go for it!

When you've finished, take a moment to reflect on what you've written. Did you find this exercise easy or hard to do?

Having been quite carefree with your cash up until the point where you've won the lotto, how likely do you think you would be to look after it properly when a big stash appears, seemingly out of nowhere?

1) Highly likely
2) Impossible to say
3) Not very likely at all

What's your reason for this answer?

If you answered highly likely here, your optimism and positive outlook are admirable. Of course there's no one-size-fits-all response to anything that involves the billions of people on the planet. We can be unpredictable. Overall, though, the chances of us swinging from money mishap to money mogul overnight are slim.

But what if I said there was a way to virtually guarantee you'd put yourself in the best possible position to manage and, most importantly, keep your cash? There's nothing fancy or new about this method. You may even find that some of the adults you know are already using this method to some degree, even if it exists solely in their heads rather than on paper.

It's called a *drum roll please*... **BUDGET**.

OK I hear you, it's not exactly the most exciting part of your money-management glow-up is it?

I get that it's nowhere near as fancy as coming up with ways to earn your own money and then to grow it for future use. But trust me when I say, on the road to developing your Royal Money Mindset and managing your money like a queen, this is one of the first and most important steps.

But what is a budget? Simply, a budget is an organizer for your money.

You know those timetables you have that help you to manage your school schedule so you know which class is happening when, with whom, and where? Well, used effectively, your budget is just like that.

Over time you come to know your school schedule like the back of your hand. You don't need to constantly dig it out to check where you should be next period because it just becomes second nature to you. Setting a solid budget is one of the best ways to make sure that you are in control of your money rather than your money controlling you.

Here are some of the other parallels between these two handy ways to manage your life:

SCHOOL SCHEDULE

- Manage your school diary
- Says where you should be when
- Lets you know what you will be studying
- Tells you who will be teaching your lesson
- Helps you identify gaps in your schedule for studying/leisure

BUDGET

- Manage your money diary
- Says where your money should be when
- Lets you know what your money is being spent on
- Tells you who your money is being spent with (e.g. different stores)
- Helps you identify where you might be spending more than you're saving or other imbalances

Can you imagine the chaos that unfolds at the start of the school year when students are unclear about where they need to be? Imagine the possible outcomes.

Students turning up to the wrong class, not paying attention, and then sitting all the way through and then realizing they're meant to be in math.

Teachers frustrated that you failed to file your homework on time because you didn't know it was due that day.

And perhaps one of my favorites (or not): missing your free period at school, which you could have used to get a headstart on your homework, so you don't *actually* have to do it at home, go for a run, or even, ssshhh, have a lie in.

You see what I mean? **CHAOS.**

The same principles apply to our financial life.

Here are three scenarios that could cause financial mayhem in your life:

1) It's your friend's birthday and you're all going to the movies. A trip like this usually costs you about $20 but you bought a couple of spontaneous bubble teas on your way home from school last week so your available spending money is now $5.32.

*2) You've worked hard all summer washing the neighbors' cars, mowing lawns, and you even built a new website for your aunt's cake-making business. You *think* you made a lot of money. But you haven't really been tracking it so now you're not quite sure whether you've made enough to buy that new laptop after all or whether you need to do a couple more jobs to make up the difference.*

3) You've decided to do a spending challenge and see whether you can massively cut your spending, because you're fed up of running out of cash by the end of the week. Only you have no way of knowing what you've been spending because you have no system for doing so, it's become a bit of a free-for-all where that's concerned.

Do you see how a lack of clarity, foresight, and, dare I say it again, budget, can totally kill the vibe?

As the saying goes: fail to plan, plan to fail.

Savage, I know, but how else are we going to learn?

So now we know why we need a budget, how exactly do we set one?

Well a good place to start is to understand the different options available to you. Over the following few pages we'll talk about three, starting with the most intense.

1.
ZERO SUM

The zero-sum method is the most detailed budgeting method there is, in that it requires an extreme level of precision around your spending habits.

Let's say you receive an allowance of $20 a week, delivered straight into your bank account or, if you have a job (whoopie!) then your paycheck. As soon as you receive it, you split it up to the nearest [insert your local currency here], across the different activities that require you to spend your money. In essence: every cent has its place.

The good news is that the level of detail involved with this method means you will be able to **forecast or predict** precisely what you expect to be spending in the week or month ahead. **That way you should never run out of money.**

The bad news is that it can be a bit of a problem if something unexpected comes up or you'd just like to do something you wouldn't otherwise be doing.

It also assumes that you actually know, to that level of detail, what you spend on repeatedly in the first place.

Who this might be good for: people who are extremely organized and who like things in order at all times. For example: Is your room permanently tidy with everything in place? Is your social diary booked way in advance? Does chaos give you a major headache? Then this one may be for you!

2.
ENVELOPE METHOD

Imagine having some multi-colored envelopes, labeled with different categories based on your average monthly spend. You would then carve up your cash each week or month and distribute it across the different envelopes.

Are you regularly forking out for various sports club subscriptions? Magazines? Books? Toiletries? Contact lenses? Whatever it is you are spending on consistently would warrant its very own envelope.

Done well, this method would mean that there are **no surprises** when it comes to your money, because **you will have accounted for every cent in advance.**

As your experience and comfort with using this method grow, you'll be able to look for clues in your own spending patterns and behaviors, a bit like being a private investigator in your own life, and quickly identify if something's not quite right.

The downside is that it requires you to be fairly confident that you can commit to the spending categories you set for yourself at the start of your budgeting period, whether it's the week or a month.

Although this is a good discipline overall, there will inevitably be those times when you just want to be able to do something completely spontaneously. While doing this from time to time is perhaps no bad thing, the envelope approach to budgeting may not offer the flexibility to do this with ease. Instead, you could end up robbing Petra to pay Paula (or whatever the saying is) or, in other words, borrowing from one envelope to top up another, which undermines the whole thing entirely.

Who this might be good for: people who prefer to spend their money in cash. It's also for you if you find yourself running out of money all the time and can't pinpoint where it's gone!

3.

THE 50/30/20 METHOD

OK so the final method is the one that offers you the most flexibility around how you manage your money. The 50/30/20 method is a way of categorizing your cash according to three main areas: your needs (50%), your wants (30%), and savings and investments (20%).

Here's how it might look in practice:

This is how your chart might look in twenty years time:

Savings!
Investments

Needs
• Mortgage/rent
• Gas/electricity
• Groceries

Wants
• Yoga classes
• Monthly massage/facial

The beauty of this approach is the **flexibility** it gives you. Whilst it offers a great way to organize how you intend to spend your money on a very basic level, it does not hold you to an extreme level of precision around how that money is spent. Instead it offers broad guidelines to follow which you can adjust to suit your needs.

For example, if you live at home with family who are currently footing the bill for the majority of your needs, then that frees you up to reserve more of your money for savings while you still can. In that instance, 50/30/20 for you might instead look more like 20/30/50.

Conversely, if you've just started driving lessons, for example, and are paying for them yourself, then your wants category might be more than 30% for the time being, and your split might instead look like 20/60/20.

The upside of this is that it provides a framework for how you conserve your cash without being overbearing.

Do be aware, though, that it also requires a hefty amount of self-discipline from you too. There's just no getting around that.

It's a bit like when you get to your lesson at school, realize the teacher isn't there and in that instant have to make a decision about what to do next. Do you a) spend a few minutes gabbing with your friend before the two of you whip out your notebooks and catch up on homework or recap on the previous lesson or b) spend the entire time talking and laughing, wasting your opportunity to get a headstart.

If you answered b) this method is not for you!

Who this might be good for: those of you that have a good grasp of your finances already and trust yourself to make savvy money moves the majority of the time.

ACTIVITY

Think about each category carefully. Which one of these budgeting methods appeals most to you? Do you think you're orderly enough to go with the zero-sum method? Perhaps the envelope method sounds more up your alley? Maybe you like the flexibility of the 50/30/20 method? Why does your chosen one appeal to you? Write down the reason for your choice.

Next make a list of all the things you spend on each month (at this stage don't focus so much on who is paying the bill–it's fine for this to be your parents or carers). Apply one of the methods above to your current spending. Set a time frame that you want to trial this out for (Tip: aim for at least one month to give yourself time to figure it out.)

What have you discovered about yourself through this process? Based on your evaluation do one of these things: a) Keep, b) Tweak, c) Ditch and switch!

Why is this a core part of your Royal Money Mindset?

Because learning this principle when you're managing a few dollars will mean that managing thousands or millions in the future will be a breeze.

Just as you would take driving lessons before leaping behind the steering wheel for the first time, practicing how to manage and budget in small amounts is a great way to train yourself to be disciplined enough to manage larger amounts with ease.

The principles of budgeting give us life lessons that extend beyond just how we manage our money—the discipline and attention to detail required to make our budgets work also applies to how we run our lives. If you can crack this part of your money management early, you'll unlock one of the secrets to long-term success and happiness.

CROWN JEWELS

So now you know how budgeting forms part of your money maven toolkit. Here are five key things to remember.

1.

Learning how to keep the money you make is equally as important as how much you make.

2.

A budget is a money-management tool that helps you to organize your money. It is not a stick to beat yourself with or a kind of financial jail. Instead it is a way to free yourself from money worries and uncertainty.

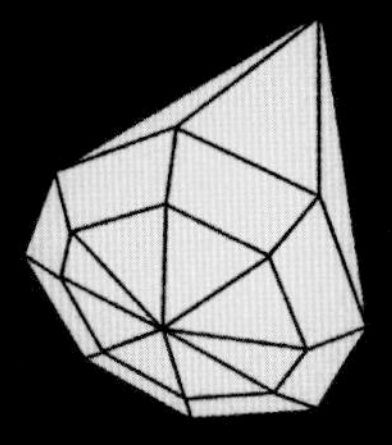

3.

Budgeting is key to setting solid financial foundations. Getting it right now gives you a massive headstart for the future.

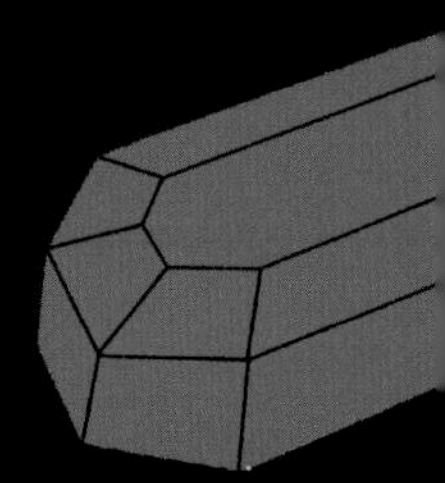

4.

There are a number of budget options to choose from—pick one that works best for you and don't be afraid to experiment.

5.

Remember to carve out space for the things you enjoy in your budget, however big or small.

CHAPTER FOUR

THERE'S NO BETTER MONEY THAN MONEY YOU'VE EARNED YOURSELF

So now you've got a good system for managing your money, let's have a talk about where exactly you're going to get it from in the first place.

You may be wondering why this chapter comes right after the budgeting one. Surely you need to be earning some money in the first place before you can even think about how to organize it? Well yes, but do you remember what we said at the end of the last chapter? Learning how to manage your money when you're working with small amounts or even zero, puts you in the best possible position to transition into managing larger amounts without even breaking a sweat.

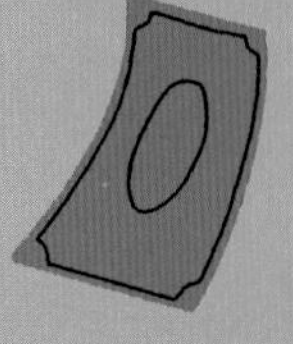

Before we go any further, let's break down some of the jargon related to getting your money.

What's the difference between income and earnings?

Income is a broad term that is used to encapsulate all money that quite literally "comes in" to your bank account, whether you've worked for it or not.

At this stage in your life, the majority of the income you've received to date will probably have come from loved ones perhaps in the form of gifts or an allowance.

Money that you earn by having a job is just one source of income you will generate over the course of your life, however, there are many others. So let's break down some of the different income sources you may already be familiar with or be generating.

You know that expression: don't put all your eggs in one basket? That's basically what is meant by diversification.

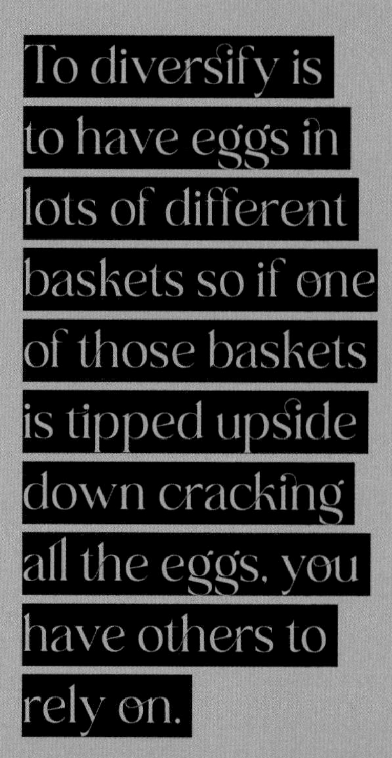

Diversification is an important term you need to start getting used to when it comes to your money, including the money you earn. We'll return to it again when we talk about investing.

Similarly, you may have heard the adults in your life talk about the value of getting a good education so you have "something to fall back on." The reason they say this is because they understand the merits of diversification. While you could happily get a job without, say, a college degree, what they want for you is to have options.

In their mind, the greater the education, the greater the number of opportunities available to you. These options in turn provide you with a greater sense of financial security, which is one of the main benefits of cultivating our Royal Money Mindset.

Your income sources are no different. Applying the principle of diversification to your income helps to provide you with a more solid financial foundation to live your very best life as an adult. But which ones are available to you? For now, let's focus on the following four:

1) Earned income: money that you earn by having a job.

2) Business income: money that you earn from customers by offering them a product or service.

3) Interest income: money that you earn on savings held in a financial institution such as a bank or credit union.

4) Gifted income: money that you receive from loved ones e.g. as an allowance, or as presents, perhaps for excellent grades, a birthday or other occasion.

We're going to focus on the first two in this chapter.

EARNED INCOME

Just like passing your driving test, going away to college or even going on your first overnight school trip away from home, getting a job as a young adult is one of the most thrilling milestones you'll experience.

Why? Because it's the first time you will get a taste of financial independence and what it means to spend money you have earned yourself purely through your own efforts.

For those of us who are lucky enough to have received a regular allowance, that is, gifted income, the idea of receiving cash to spend as you wish is nothing new. But the feel-good factor that comes from earning it yourself, is unrivaled.

FINDING WHAT YOU LOVE TO DO AND BEING PAID FOR IT

Remember, whether you are running your own business or are employed by one, in both cases you are exchanging your time for money. Well duh, I hear you say. This is a no-brainer.

But just think about the value of time for a moment. What sort of price would you put on yours?

For most of us, it can be a difficult concept to grasp. But a good starting point would be to reflect on what else you might be doing with that time. That is, an hour spent doing something that fills you with joy, doesn't harm others, teaches you something new, or maybe helps someone else is probably an hour well spent.

This doesn't mean abandoning everything you don't like or aren't very good at either. So much of our development as humans comes from discovering new things about ourselves and the world we live in. But understanding that there are options for how you use your time and that you have the power to choose as you get older, or even now, should help you be ruthless about how you manage yours.

There's a reason it's referred to as "spending time"—it is one of our most precious commodities and one that we cannot get back after it has gone. Understanding the personal cost to us in spending our time one way over another and whether or not it's worth it overall when we look at what we gained, can help us really focus on how to use ours wisely.

ACTIVITY

Do a quick poll of the grown-ups you live with and ask them what value or price tag they would put on one hour of their time. Make a note of your findings. Is it higher or lower than you expected?

Whether or not we can put a specific value on our time, it's fair to say that most of us would give it a fairly high price.

So it stands to reason, then, that whatever we trade our time for in exchange for money, we need to make sure we feel good about the trade based on whether or not it meets one of a range of personal benefits Here are some to start you off.

Checklist: How should your job benefit you?

- Pay you a fair wage.
- Teach you something new.
- Boost your mood.
- Help you to find out what you might like to do in your future career.
- Give you an opportunity to try and fail safely.

ACTIVITY

What are your top three priorities in finding a job? Get your notebook back out and make a list for yourself.

Now you're clear on what is important to you in finding a job, all you need to do is start looking! But where to begin? I think that the best place to start is to think about what you enjoy doing.

- What are your hobbies/interests?

- Do you have a favorite diner or restaurant that might need serving staff?

- Where do you do your shopping? Do you accompany your parents to do the grocery store every weekend, do you have a favorite clothes store?

Whatever it is, when you start job hunting, look for clues in your everyday life, to guide you to something you'll enjoy. This way you'll give yourself a fighting chance of actually loving what you do as well as the prospect of staff discounts at one of your favorite places, which is a nice bonus!

Business income

Alternatively, if you aren't quite old enough to get a job in a company just yet, or if you are a budding entrepreneur at heart and have always loved the idea of running your own business, then here are some options to get you started.

ACTIVITY

What else can you think of to add to the list on the previous page? Jot down some other ideas you've been pondering over, or something you've already set up.

By now you should have a good idea of the different income sources available to you. Perhaps you're already earning your own money through selling your services in one of the examples listed above or via another business venture, or you may have secured your first job.

ACTIVITY

Make a list of your income sources using the categories below. Grab a piece of paper or notebook and copy the chart below. My money comes from...

	%
Gifted	
Business	
Interest	
Earned	

OK so let's reset.

You've got the job, set up the business, or you've made a plan of action to do either or both!
You've taken an important step on the journey to financial independence as a young woman.
This is a big deal and should be celebrated.
But of course we're not going to leave it there.

The art of negotiating

One of the requirements for gaining a Royal Money Mindset is having the confidence to speak up for ourselves in all aspects of our lives, including our cash.

Sometimes, this may require you to negotiate with other people to make sure they see your true value clearly.

Before we go on, though, I need to let you know one very important thing that I want you to remember forever:

What you are paid is not, and will never be, an indicator of your worth as a person.

There is no amount of money that could ever reflect your true value as a friend, daughter, sister, niece, etc.

That said, part of having a Royal Money Mindset is making sure that you are paid appropriately for your skills and experience based on what the market rate is, and not a cent less.

ACTIVITY

Let's start by reminding ourselves of what would make us an asset to any workplace in the first place. What are some of the best things about being you? Write down your top five. Here's an example to get you started:

1. I do what I say I will do.
2. I'm always on time.
3. I'm a good friend.
4. I'm careful with money.
5. I'm energetic and upbeat.

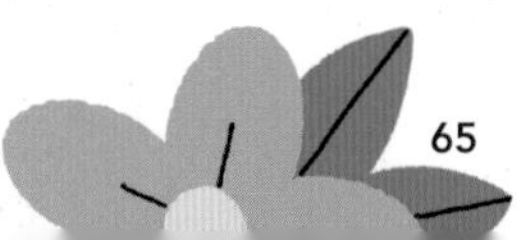

Here's how they translate into powerful skills that would benefit your employer or your customers.

See? You already possess so many valuable qualities that could make a big difference to a company. So now you just need to get them to see that. That's where negotiating comes in.

Negotiation is the art of exchanging something of value with someone who has made you an offer, so you get a better deal. And guess what? You've probably been doing this since you were a baby.

Don't believe me? Just look at some of the small children you know. Let's say you offer them a piece of fruit. They might ask for two which you say yes to as long as they sit nicely and behave themselves.

Chances are you do this in your home today too. Let's say a family member offers you $20 to wash all the family cars. You might negotiate more money by saying you'll give them a polish as well as a wash for an additional $10. If the adult agrees, that's a successful negotiation.

But it doesn't always have to be money. You might negotiate to stay longer at your friend's house if you get all your homework done by a certain time. Or to stay up later than usual to watch your favorite new show on Netflix, provided you agree to wake up early enough to take your sister to her Saturday morning music lesson.

ACTIVITY

What else can you negotiate for at home? Write down a couple of examples in your notebook or on a piece of paper. When you start work, you might be negotiating for:

1. Certain days of the week that you'll work.

2. Fewer or greater number of working hours around your other commitments such as school or college.

3. A different department or team if you think your skills would be better used there.

Your mission is to get your new employer to see things your way and either be willing to agree to your requests directly or accept a trade.

Remember that in a negotiation you could receive one of three possible responses:

A COMPROMISE POSITION WHERE YOU AND YOUR NEGOTIATING PARTNER AGREE TO MEET IN THE MIDDLE AND YOU BOTH GIVE UP SOMETHING TO PLEASE THE OTHER PERSON.

Which one do you think leads to the best possible outcome for everyone involved and why?

Why is this such a big deal? Three words: gender pay gap.

Say you are offered a Saturday job in a diner but you'd applied to work the whole weekend to increase your pay (you're saving towards a specific goal). The diner owner might say they don't have any need for an additional person to work for the whole day on a Sunday, but that she'd be happy to offer you some extra hours to cover the morning.

While you don't receive the full day you'd hoped for, you are still in a better position to the offer you first received and so you happily accept. By speaking up and making your wishes clear, you give yourself a chance of getting what you truly want rather than just accepting the first offer you receive, particularly if it's not quite right for you.

THIS IS THE POWER OF NEGOTIATION.

As you get older this negotiation may change to improved pay and better employee benefits. Like more days of holiday, for example.

This may not be something you're familiar with but it's something you need to be aware of as you enter adulthood. Mainly so you can lend your voice to the campaign to squash this once and for all.

In short, the gender pay gap refers to a situation in which **women are paid less than men at work,** a situation that could cost us millions over the course of our working lives.

A number of factors can cause this problem. But one of the actions we can take to combat this is to be our own cheerleaders and to speak up for ourselves at work, negotiating every step of the way.

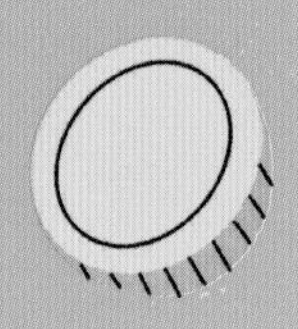

Here are some of the other dos and don'ts to bear in mind when you're starting your very first job.

DOS

- Do speak up.
- Do set boundaries.
- Do be realistic—not all work is fun. That's just the way it goes. But neither should it be horrific either. Balance is key.
- Do be willing to learn from others.
- Do be willing to get your hands dirty.

DON'TS

- Don't shrink your personality.
- Don't undervalue your time or talents.
- Don't underestimate your self-worth—where you start is not where you will finish.
- Don't make unrealistic demands.
- Don't mistake rudeness for assertiveness. Be respectful.

CROWN JEWELS

Let's round up our five key things to remember.

1.
Earning our own money is one of the best ways to achieve financial independence.

2.
There are lots of different sources of income—think about how you can diversify yours as you get older so you don't put all your eggs in one basket.

3.
The gender pay gap currently means women earn less than men over their lifetimes—it's important that you speak up to make sure you're paid fairly for your skills and talents.

4.
What you are paid is in no way linked to your worth as a person. You already have so many winning qualities to offer—be your own cheerleader!

5.
Your time is one of your most valuable commodities and can never be replaced once it's gone—exchange yours for something that helps you to grow and develop as well as paying you. Your first job doesn't have to be your dream job but remember where you start is not where you

CHAPTER FIVE

INVESTING 101: SLOW AND STEADY WINS THE RACE

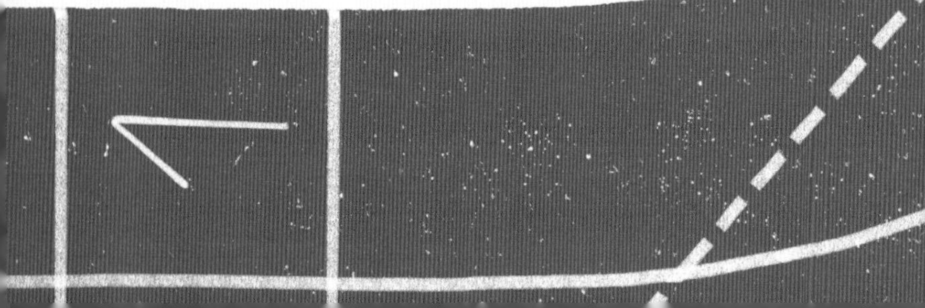

In the last chapter we talked about how to earn money of our own. Once we've earned it, the next question of course is, what on Earth do we do with it? Spoiler alert—for the avoidance of doubt, spending it all isn't the answer.

This is where investing comes in.

But first things first, what is investing? And what's the difference between this and regular cash saving?

Saving vs investing

Cash saving involves you putting money aside for use at a later date. Do you remember what we said about deferred gratification in chapter two? This is exactly that. Typically we put our cash savings in a savings account held by a financial institution such as a bank or credit union, though many of us started with a money box!

In exchange for us entrusting these banks with our cash, we receive "interest" on the total amount held. This measure, usually shown as a percentage (say 2 or 3%) is how much our money grows. This growth is effectively extra cash—a reward for our patience.

Saving is an easy to understand and important way to preserve your cash for a rainy day or even a specific goal like a car or to travel.

Keeping a stash of cash saved is a real boss move. As you get older and move into your own place, sometimes life will throw you a lemon. There's nothing we can do about that, but what we can do is manage our response to it. Instead of being hit in the face, waking up dazed and wondering what's just happened, we want to catch it, squeeze it, and make delicious lemonade. That's what having an emergency saving fund will help you do.

Here are some examples:

- Your boiler breaks down in the middle of the coldest winter on record and you urgently need to get a replacement.

- You realize your job is making you sick with stress and you need to leave to give you the breathing space to look for a new one.

- You're living abroad and need to book flights quickly to get home for a family emergency.

ACTIVITY

What other emergencies might come up that you need a special savings pot to cover? Having an idea of what these things might be is a great way to make them a priority in your planning by assessing the impact on you and your quality of life if you didn't have the cash to cover them. However, sadly saving isn't always completely risk-free.

THE SILENT ASSASSIN

Let's say you put $100 into a savings account paying 2% interest each year. But the cost of living, which includes things like groceries, gas, as well as home energy, is rising at 3% each year. In this example, your cash is simply not able to keep up. Without even realizing it, the value of your savings, in terms of what your money can buy, is slowly dwindling over time. This is known as **inflation** and it's a bit of a silent assassin, creeping up and gulping up your cash when you're not looking.

One of the best ways to manage the impact of inflation is to keep track of what's happening with the money you save and spend by:

1) Monitoring the average cost of day-to-day household purchases, across the country as well as your household. In the US, this is measured by a Consumer Price Index (CPI) and is reported on by the US Bureau of Labor Statistics (BLS).

2) Making sure that the interest you're generating on your savings is at a higher percentage than the current rate of inflation. If it isn't, then what might have seemed a risk-free, easy way to save your cash might suddenly appear more risky than you first thought.

NO PAIN, NO GAIN

Alternatively, you could consider other ways of preserving and growing your cash that involve more risk, but have the potential for greater return over time, staying one step ahead of inflation along the way. This is known as the risk-reward trade-off. The idea of generating the best return on your cash, while exposing it to the least amount of danger or risk.

Investing is an example of this. In its simplest form, investing involves you putting your cash into "assets" that might generate even more cash for you in the future by accelerating the speed of growth. The main difference between these assets is the potential for reward based on the level of risk you are willing to take with your cash.

Your assets are an important weapon in your toolkit when it comes to securing your financial future and funding the life of your dreams. So what kinds of assets are there?

Assets come in a number of different categories. Let's take a look at some of the most common kinds.

- Stock-market investments
- Fine art
- Antiques
- Jewelery
- Real estate
- Precious metals (gold or silver for example)
- Cryptocurrencies and NFTs (digital art)
- You!

Bet you didn't expect to see yourself feature in a line up of valuable assets to invest in! Before we get back to some of the more financial categories of investment, let's talk about ourselves a bit. If you recall, our definition of investing is putting our cash into anything that we expect will generate more cash for us in the future. But there's something equally as valuable, if not more valuable than cash, that we can also invest. Can you think of what this is?

Time and money regularly come up as two of the most valuable resources that, when managed correctly, can have a massive impact on our quality of life.

Imagine how much time you've spent at school since you first started there. It's probably somewhere in the region of ten or so years. The amount of knowledge you have accumulated in that time is incalculable.

Now imagine that all of that knowledge has blossomed into new skills and built up over time. Without you even realizing it, the combined total of everything you've learned packs a mighty punch when applied to areas in which you excel. So your:

- [ ] time-management skills
- [ ] problem solving
- [ ] negotiating and persuasion
- [ ] ability to speak other languages to help you communicate with others
- [ ] ability to communicate clearly full stop
- [ ] understanding and experience of our diverse world and cultures as a result of any travel you have undertaken…

… all of these skills contribute to the infinite value that you add to the world over the course of your life and enhance your biggest asset by far: **YOU.**

UNDERSTANDING THIS PRINCIPLE IS IMPORTANT.

Here's why:

1) Because there may be times in our lives that we find we are not in a position to add to our financial assets but that doesn't mean we have no assets at all: **remember our worth as individuals far exceeds any financial worth we might generate.**

2) When we recognize that we are our own biggest asset by far, we start to treat ourselves with way more care and attention. Say you get a pair of limited edition Nike Air Jordans for Christmas. There are only 100 pairs of these shoes in the world. You're not going to be wearing them for a kick-around in the park, are you? You'll probably handle them with such extreme love and respect that your parents will be in awe. That's the same kind of treatment you owe yourself.

3) If we had to tie them to a monetary value, then guess what? The skills that you build on daily, as your knowledge and experience grow, are what will help you to earn the money that you can use elsewhere in your life.

So yeah, we're a big deal as far as assets go.

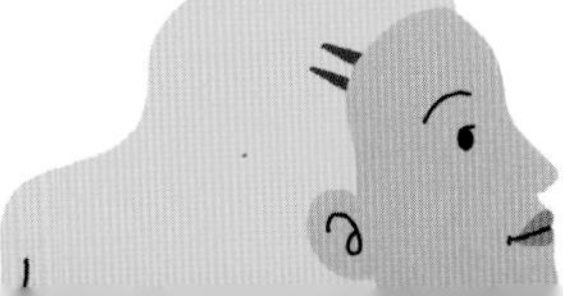

But what about some other assets that we can invest in? Let's shine a spotlight on one of the oldest forms of investing, specifically the stock market and one of the newest, cryptocurrencies.

THE STOCK MARKET

Some of you may have seen movies in which stock-market investing is depicted as a rollercoaster ride of swinging highs and lows, market crashes, people frantically running around in offices shouting into cell phones and well... pandemonium.

The reality, however, is a little more pedestrian than that for the vast majority of us. It's a bit more of a marathon than a sprint. This is because the best way to maximize those returns is to hold your nerve and be willing to stay in the market and remain invested for a long time. Any attempt to outsmart the market and get rich quick is a losing game, regardless of what you may see on TikTok.

It's in this slow, steady state that we will focus our investing efforts. Why? Because while it may not seem as exciting as the high-octane images sensationalized by Hollywood (don't get me wrong, I love those movies too, the more dramatic the better), taking baby steps and building up over time is one of the best ways to make investment decisions we feel happy with—ones that won't keep us awake at night with anxiety.

But if we want to invest in the stock market, first we need to know what we're doing.

DID YOU KNOW?

DESPITE MEN OUTPACING WOMEN WHEN IT COMES TO MAKING THE DECISION TO START INVESTING, WHEN WE DO GET GOING, THE RETURNS WE GENERATE ARE, ON AVERAGE, HIGHER THAN OUR MALE FRIENDS. ANOTHER GREAT REMINDER TO BELIEVE IN YOURSELF AND YOUR ABILITIES. YOU'VE GOT THIS!

(SOURCE: WARWICK BUSINESS SCHOOL.)

The stock market is essentially an index or list, of companies that are publicly traded. This means that members of the general public, like you and me, can buy shares in them and that we are, in essence, part owners of those companies we have shares in.

In contrast, private companies do not raise money from the general public. Shares in those companies are typically owned by a combination of the directors of those companies and a small number of others, which may include staff, for example. Any local family business that you know of is a good example of this, but private companies vary in size and scope.

HOW DO YOU BUY THEM?

The two main ways you can invest in the stock market, are either through:

- Individual shares, or
- Investment funds

The best way to think about this is to imagine candy bars. An investment in individual company shares is essentially the equivalent of buying a Snickers or a Twix. But what if you wanted a Snickers and a Twix and a Kit Kat and... you get the point. If you're someone that values variety, and as an investor you totally should, then a fund is a great way to achieve this.

ACTIVITY

Based on our candy bar analogy, which of the following statements do you think best describes one of the main principles of investing through funds:

1) Don't put all your eggs in one basket.
2) What goes up must come down.
3) The winner takes it all.

If you picked the first statement, you'd be correct. This principle, known as diversification, is an important one to remember when it comes to investing.

Diversification is your secret weapon when it comes to keeping your risk levels as low as possible, while at the same time keeping the money you make from your investments, otherwise known as returns, as high as possible.

This means that if one of the companies in your investment fund bombs, all is not lost. As long as the other companies in the fund do well, your money still has the opportunity to grow and offset or cancel out the loss from the ones that are doing badly.

This is what is meant by "fund performance." It's a bit like getting your report card that sets out how well you're doing each school year. Just as you and your parents will be paying close attention to your grades or academic performance, investors, just like you, also monitor their investment performance too.

This brings us on to another important investment concept: **return on investment, otherwise known as ROI.**

Very simply, this is a way of measuring how well your investment is doing. This is usually depicted in percentage terms to make it easy to compare it with other investments.

To illustrate this, let's go back to your report card. By now you've probably already been assessed at least once to check how well you're doing against other young people your age in your school. One of the factors contributing to your final grade will be how well you perform against national average grades as well as how much time and effort you put into acing the tests.

In this context, your investment from an academic standpoint would be equivalent to your study time and your return would be your grade. When it comes to your money, your investment would be the amount of cash you put into each fund while your return would be how well the companies your fund is invested in did against other companies in its industry or sector, measured as a percentage.

ACTIVITY

Do you have a favorite clothes store, tech company, or brand of trainers? Why not ask for a share in that company for your birthday gift instead of the physical item itself. Fancy Air Jordans? Request a Nike share. Tech fan? How about shares in Apple?

While the gadget or trainers will give the immediate gratification we talked about in chapter two (until a newer model comes out and yours becomes obsolete), the share could grow in value over time so you benefit from even greater returns in the long run. Talk about the gift that keeps on giving! (If you can though, get the trainers too—it is your birthday after all!)

CRYPTOCURRENCIES

The best way to describe cryptos, is to think of them as a digital currency in contrast with the physical currency, or cash, you might have in your purse. It is not to be confused with paying for things with a bank card or another type of digital payment, via your smartphone, for example. While these payments are virtual too in that they are enabled by technology, the actual source of the payment is still the physical cash you have you in your account, typically held in a bank.

With cryptos, physical cash is swapped for a new currency that only exists online, there is no bank or government behind it, unlike the money in our wallets.

ACTIVITY

Take a look at a banknote and read the small print on it to see where it was issued. What can you find out?

Typically it will have a picture of a national hero or figure of public interest, such as a former country leader, on it, as well as details of the government or institution that is responsible for issuing the cash or physically printing it. In the US, for example, all banknotes will have "The United States of America" on them - with different notes featuring the faces of different past presidents.

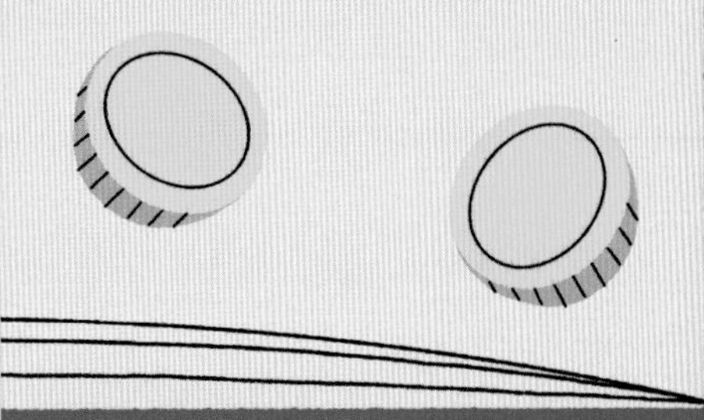

Cryptocurrency is built on "blockchain," which, in simple terms, is a way of recording huge amounts of data in blocks that digitally record transactions securely, making them difficult to hack. Blockchain can also be used to record NFT ownership.

It is based on a technology called "cryptography," which encrypts or disguises data to make it secret so transactions using cryptocurrency are anonymous.

Examples of cryptocurrencies that you may have heard of are Bitcoin or Ethereum but there are tons of others.

Now here's the real talk: investing in cryptos is not for the fainthearted. It is one of the riskiest categories of investment that exists today with a number of unknowns. This doesn't mean you should avoid it completely.

But, it's important to be knowledgeable about all your options so you can decide what decisions to make in the future.

However, don't be enticed by celebrities or influencers telling you why it's the best place for your money—let your Royal Money Mindset be your guide, do your research and don't follow the crowd if it doesn't make sense to you.

SPOTLIGHT ON NFTS

A quick word on NFTs while we're here—think of these as digital versions of real-life items, often collectibles like art, music, even video games, that can be invested in with cryptocurrencies. They are stored in a blockchain which, due to the cryptography described above, reduces the chance of fraud as each digital asset or token has a unique identifier linked to its owner.

If you could turn any collectors' item into an NFT, which one would you choose and why? Of course stock-market investing is not the only place for your cash. Other categories of investment include:

- Bonds: a form of investment that pays a regular rate of interest issued by governments or companies around the world.

- Commodities: such as oil, gold, gems.

- Real estate: property that pays you rental income. This could be commercial property like stores, or residential property like houses or flats.

- Cryptocurrencies and NFTs: digital currencies like Bitcoin or Ethereum as well as digital art that can be traded like physical currencies (such as dollars or pounds).

These different investment types all have varying degrees of risk attached to them and perform differently in terms of the likely rate of return you can expect to receive.

This is why diversification is so important: putting all of your money into the highest risk investments you can find is unwise, but then so is having no risk attached to your investment at all.

Finding the right balance for you and your investment goals is key.

BUT WHERE TO BEGIN?

I hope by now you're beginning to be interested in starting your own investment portfolio when the time is right—your personal, diversified collection of all your assets. Before you begin, here is a checklist to consider.

PRE-INVESTING CHECKLIST

1) UNDERSTANDING OF WHAT YOU ARE INVESTING IN AND THE RISKS

Ever heard the expression "knowledge is power?" Well there are few places it could be more powerful than when it comes to your cash. One thing we're absolutely not going to do is start putting our money into things we don't understand. If having a Royal Money Mindset means being in control of our cash, well this is the opposite of that.

2) CAPACITY FOR RISK

OK, so now you understand what you're investing in, can you afford to take on the risks associated with choosing that investment? Or, in other words, if the investment went up in smoke completely taking all of your money with it, how much would this compromise how you currently live? If making this investment would make your financial foundations wobbly then that's a good reason to think again, at least temporarily.

3) RISK APPETITE

Are you someone that finds comfort in certainty (or as close to certainty as possible) or do you prefer the excitement of the unknown? Knowing how you respond to unpredictability is a key factor in deciding when and where to invest your money. The last thing you want to do is invest in something that will give you sleepless nights with worry.

4) WHAT MATTERS MOST TO YOU

Do you have strong values or ethics that influence how you live your life on a day-to-day basis? If so your investments should reflect that. Perhaps you'd prefer to invest only in green companies, or those that don't sell tobacco or alcohol. Whatever it is, be clear on your guiding principles and make sure your investments match.

5) INVESTMENT OBJECTIVE

Knowing whether you're investing for a specific goal, to be realized within a specific timeframe, vs having a more general goal to grow your cash for an undefined point in the future, could help narrow down which investments are right for you. Being clear on this early is a real Royal move.

WHERE TO BEGIN

Due to the risks associated with investing, you have to be over eighteen to start. That doesn't mean you can't still get involved at a younger age. Ask your parents for help identifying the options that are available to you at your age. If they're already saving or investing on your behalf, then great, you've got a headstart! Now's the time to learn more about where your money is going.

If you're starting from scratch, then you have a blank canvas! What are some of your goals? Where would you like to invest in the future? When would you like to begin? Start putting together a little plan and doing your research so, as soon as the time is right, you're ready to go!

CROWN JEWELS

So now you have an idea of what investing is all about and some of the considerations you need to make before you build your own winning portfolio! Here's a recap of some of the key things to remember.

1. Cash saving and stock-market investing are distinct but important parts of a well-managed financial plan.

2. Inflation is a silent assassin when it comes to your cash and could mean that the value of your money over time is depleted. Keep track of this if your money is held in a savings account.

3. Investing is a great way to grow your money but you must understand the risks.

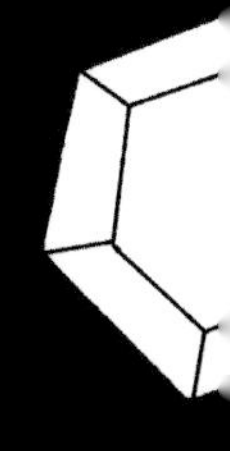

4. When women do invest we smash it—trust yourself!

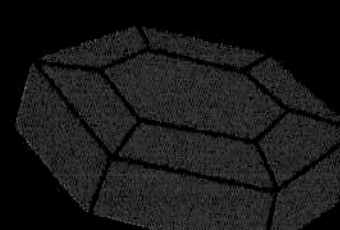

5. Diversification is your secret weapon when it comes to trying to maximize how much you can grow your money without putting it in danger of being lost due to excessive risk.

CHAPTER SIX

YOU CONTROL YOUR MONEY, YOUR MONEY DOESN'T CONTROL YOU

Having a Royal Money Mindset is not just about living the life of a queen, though that is a huge part of it.

In some ways, an even bigger part of it is the responsibility that comes from leading by example and managing your money in a way that is befitting of a young woman who is clear about who she is, what contribution she intends to make in the world, and how important it is to have financial foundations built on concrete and not on sand.

To do this means not leaving anything to chance or whim. It means cultivating positive habits that will help us make powerful financial decisions on autopilot. And it means putting the right systems in place to make sure those decisions are executed to perfection each and every time.

Which direction are your subconscious thoughts taking you?

In the first chapter we talked about some of the money scripts you might have inherited so far. These scripts influence the relationship we have with money in adult life without us even realizing it.

But did you know that children form their earliest money habits from as early as the age of seven? This means that at a time when you were probably busily planning play dates or getting your clothes dirty in your local activity park, you'd already started developing a money personality. One that would potentially underpin everything you do for the rest of your life. No big deal.
(Source: Research by Cambridge University.)

So how do you know whether your money habits could do with a tune up?

Well, first of all, we need to take a step back and return to our mindset. Or, in other words, the collection of thoughts and feelings that influence our behavior. Lots of us already have healthy, positive mindsets when it comes to money and we need to just keep on doing what we're doing, checking in with ourselves periodically to make sure we're still on track.

But for those of us that need to change course, where on earth do you even start? If you're asking this question, here's a quick activity to integrate into your daily routine.

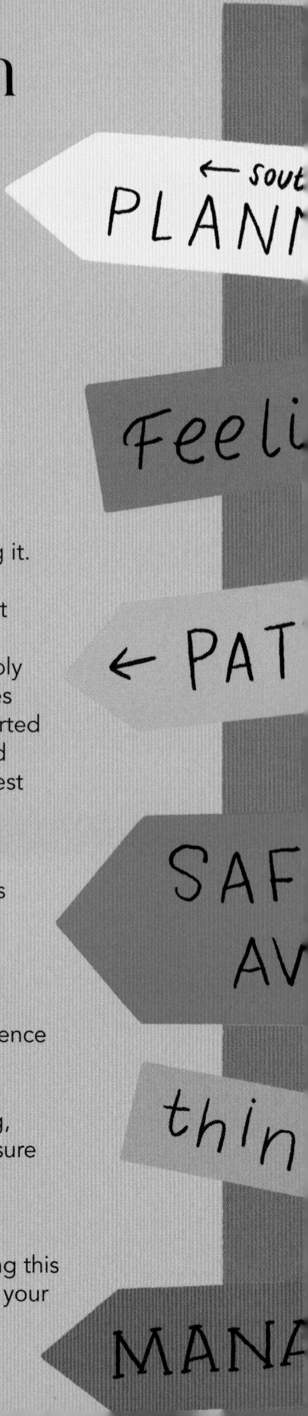

ACTIVITY

What is your money behavior telling you?
Carry out the following activity to find out.

Step 1: keep a daily money planner for a month and write down what you spend, when, why, and with whom.

Step 2: reflect on how money makes you feel. Which words or thoughts come up consistently when you think about money and most importantly, why? Do you feel excited? In control? Anxious? Unsure? Whatever it is, write it down.

Step 3: look for patterns or clues in your behavior. What do you notice about when your money behavior is at its best or makes you feel most proud? Who is with you? Do certain people impact you positively or negatively when it comes to money? For example, is there a spike in your spending when you receive bad news? Are you more careful with your money at month-end before pay day? Do you buy more books when your super well-read and sophisticated older cousin comes to visit? Write it down.

The reason you're doing this exercise is because the only way to make a lasting change is to have a clear idea of your starting point. Imagine asking someone for directions over your cell phone and they tell you the place you're looking for is round the corner on the left. Great, you think, nice and clear. But then as soon as you hang up you realize that without knowing anything about where you're standing and which way you're facing, "round the corner on the left" could take you in a few different directions.

Now we have a baseline, let's see if we can apply some theory.

I HAVE MORE THAN ENOUGH VS I NEVER HAVE ENOUGH

Two popular schools of thought when it comes to money are known as the "abundance or the scarcity mindset."

An abundance mindset means that you believe that not only do you have enough today, you will be able to generate more tomorrow with ease. In contrast, a scarcity mindset means that you believe there is not now, nor will there ever be enough, regardless of what you do.

So why does this matter? Well the main reason is that it impacts how we behave. And depending on which camp you fall into, it could seriously squeeze your ability to live a financially fruitful life. Let's try to apply these contrasting concepts in these different scenarios to really understand how it can alter our behavior.

SCENARIO 1

Your friend, Sofia, got the job you really wanted and will now be earning more money than you.

	ABUNDANCE	SCARCITY
THINK	I'm so pleased for Sofia, she's really shown what's possible. If she can do it, so can I!	Great, there's my best opportunity to move up the pay ladder gone just like that. There's never going to be another job like that now.
FEEL	Motivated and inspired.	Deflated and demotivated.
DO	Buy her a card to say congratulations and ask her for tips on how she did it.	Avoid all conversation about the topic and change the subject if she brings it up, missing out on the chance to pick up some useful gems.

SCENARIO 2

It's your sister Vivien's birthday and you want to get her a really nice gift. You've been saving diligently since you started your weekend job so have the money to get her something really good. Let's see how this one plays out...

	ABUNDANCE	SCARCITY
THINK	Vivien's birthday is coming up soon, where can I get her something really special?	Oh no, it's birthday season. How much is this going to cost me?
FEEL	Excited to give her something that she will absolutely love and pleased to have the money to do so after diligently saving all summer.	Anxious about the cost and its impact on your (healthy) bank balance.
DO	Check your budget and confidently make your purchase. You know you'll quickly replace the money you've spent as you've already demonstrated in the past.	Get her something cheaper than the thing she truly wants but which you hope she'll like anyway. It's the thought that counts after all, and you simply can't afford to be throwing money around even though you've got good savings.

Do you recognize anyone in your life who might fit into one of these categories?

Here's why an abundance mindset is so important when it comes to being in control of our money situation:

☺ It gives us confidence in our abilities to generate cash based on our skills, knowledge, and experience.

☺ It helps us recognize that where we start does not dictate where we will finish and that there are limitless opportunities to succeed.

☺ It means we see the joy in sharing opportunities with others, knowing that it doesn't take anything away from how talented we are.

Just consider the opposite under a scarcity mindset:

☹ A life of eternal penny-pinching even when we have the means to live more abundantly.

☹ Constant anxiety and worry about money (and everything else).

☹ A belief that our prospects in life are set in concrete and there's nothing we can do to improve so we'd better just accept things as they are and not get our hopes up.

Soul-destroying isn't it?

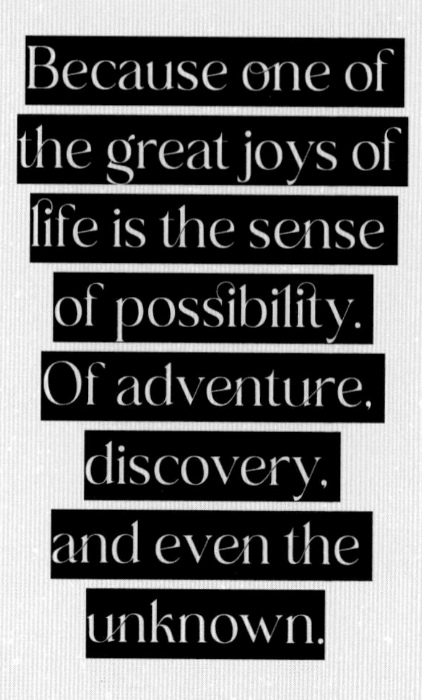

Sure, permanent uncertainty becomes unsettling after a while and nothing works without vision, planning, and execution. There may even be times when the people around you are blinded by how brightly you plan to shine and quite how big the vision for your life is, and as a result might lean on you to shrink your ambitions down to avoid being disappointed.

But this is not your job. Your job is to focus on being the absolute best you can be, recognizing you are already special just by being here, and that you have all the ingredients to go out into the world and really dazzle. Blocking your own blessings is the direct opposite of having a Royal Money Mindset. It's a hard pass from us.

Habits to last a lifetime

Now that you have an idea of how your thoughts might govern your life (and not always in a good way!) what can you do about it? Because here's the thing, your success financially or otherwise comes down to you. And not just what you are able to do once and then abandon, never to revisit again. No, the people we admire most and live the lives we most aspire to (never envy), most likely have a series of positive habits repeatedly daily that contribute to their success. Some of these habits may take the form of a daily routine which might incorporate things like this:

DAILY ROUTINE	
6 A.M.	Exercise: To stimulate the body and wake up the mind.
7 A.M.	Journaling: To plan what you'd like to achieve that day and what energy you hope to bring.
8 A.M.–12 P.M.	Work: Focus on a single project with regular breaks in-between, no social media!
12–12.15 P.M.	Social-media break.
12.15–1.15 P.M.	Lunch and walk outside.

I think you get the picture.

It doesn't mean they have to do exactly the same thing, in the same order, every single day. But by managing their day and reducing the time they spend having to decide what to do next, means they are fully in control. And the very same principle applies to our money.

Imagine having to decide every month how much to save and how much to spend? Never really knowing how much should be in your bank account? Feeling clueless on how close you are towards your pre-college girls' trip fund?

You can just imagine the outcomes. Confusion, feeling overwhelmed, and, crucially, running out of cash probably at the worst possible times.

Why? Not because you're a bad person, or don't know what you're doing. There is no question at all over your competence, otherwise you wouldn't be reading this. No, it's simply because you haven't got a good system in place for managing your money. That's it.

A systematic approach

A system is just a way of creating order or structure around something so it can be repeated over and over again with ease.

There's a great book about habits that summarizes the power of systems in a single sentence. According to its author:

"WE DON'T RISE TO THE LEVEL OF OUR GOALS,

WE FALL TO THE LEVEL OF OUR SYSTEMS."

(James Clear, *Atomic Habits*)

What a mic drop.

So, since we have no intention of "falling to the level" of anything, your system might incorporate elements of the following:

1. A scheduled monthly money date
Add a date in your diary to review your accounts. What's coming in, what's going out, anything unusual that needs reporting. This is a great habit to adopt as early as you can.

2. Regular money journalling
Here you keep a sort of diary in which you jot down what you spent each day or week. Include the choices you made when it comes to your cash such as some of the things you avoided, the things you spent money on, where you made savings. Then maybe keep a record of how you felt about these choices. Pleased? Disappointed? This is particularly good if it feels like money's just flying out of your account before you can catch it.

3. A clear budget
Have a look at the methods we discussed in chapter three and pick an approach that works best for you. Remember, a budget is not meant to be a stick to beat yourself with, but instead a way to liberate yourself from haphazard money habits and help you stay on track.

4. Separate pots for separate goals
Imagine having a massive jar of jelly beans that someone has given a good shake, and trying to sort it by color because you only want the red ones? Trying to keep your money organized into different stashes for different purposes is just like that unless it is automatically funneled into multiple pots, making it easy for you to track your progress against each one and set boundaries in your spending.

5. Automated processes
The good news is that technology has made it way easier for you to do most of this on your cell phone or laptop. All you have to do is research which apps and platforms are available to you (these will differ depending on where you live and your age) and then pick the ones that you like the best.

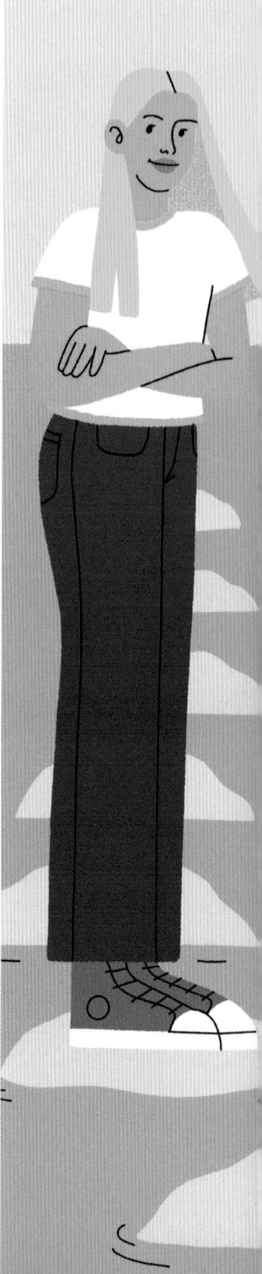

Making automation work for you—three things to look out for:

As a guide you want to start with a good bank account that has a "pots" or similar functionality to help you organize your money according to different goals.

Then you need something that can give you a clear picture of your income and outgoings and which can ping and alert you when you're getting close to zero. If it also pings you when you've got a healthy balance every month too, with some suggestions on how to make good use of your cash, even better!

Last but not least, it should automatically distribute your cash into your savings pots each month on a fixed date. This is important. Any attempt to do this manually runs the risk that we'll sabotage ourselves by a) taking a month off, b) reducing the amount we save, or c) even just forgetting. Think of it as your payment to future you. You wouldn't dream of stealing from yourself would you? Of course not. Automate the process and pay yourself first.

CROWN JEWELS

Hopefully your brain is bubbling over with some of the ways you can shift your habits and give your Royal Money Mindset a tune up, changing your behavior in the process. Here's a recap.

1. You control your money—your money doesn't control you.

2. Our financial behaviors are driven by our thoughts and feelings. Understanding how these factors influence what we do is key to making real change.

3. An abundance mindset is central to your level of financial confidence. Avoid a scarcity mindset at all costs.

4. Keeping track of what we do and looking for clues in our behavior is the first step to noticing whether we can improve.

5. Implementing positive money habits and establishing a simple system for success mean that you'll soon be managing your money on autopilot.

6. Automate your money management to avoid leaving anything to chance and pay yourself first!

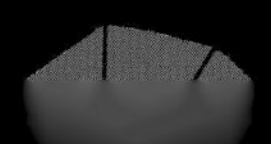

CHAPTER SEVEN

CUT YOUR CLOTH ACCORDING TO YOUR SIZE

Picture this.

You're planning a birthday outfit and decide to have something custom-made. Your bestie's mom is a seamstress, so this process is nothing new.

You go for a fitting and she measures you for your new outfit. To her surprise, just as she's finished taking the measurements, you tell her to stop everything and add a few extra inches to the sleeves, a bit more length to the pants, and two additional buttons to the jacket. None of this is necessary and will mean that the outfit will look less *haute couture* and more hot mess, but you insist on these extra add-ons because you are convinced that they will enhance the overall look.

Your friend, whose mom is making her a dress too, has an alternative plan. Instead of sizing up, she decides to size down which, although is a bit of a squeeze, she commits to in the name of fashion. She rejects the fabric her mom has selected for the dress, calling it "basic" and opts for something with a more expensive look and price tag attached to it.

Fashion *faux pas* aside (hey, we've all been there—no judgment!) there are two obvious problems with this.

1) The too large outfit will wind up costing more purely because of the additional fabric used. Simply put, the more you need, the more it costs.

2) The glitzier outfit, aside from the fact that it is too small, could also end up costing more, easily outpacing your friend's original budget because of the premium fabric used, which means the total cost of the dress has now doubled.

In each case the budget for the outfit has been agreed in advance. You've both been saving for ages to achieve the look you truly want and refused a contribution from your family members because it was important to you to that you were able to finance this yourselves. The trouble is, with both outfits now costing more than you'd planned and all the rest of the money already spent on accessories, you suddenly find yourself in a bit of a financial fix.

How on earth will you pay the difference?

Introduction to debt

Debt is a form of financial instrument where you borrow money from others in order to finance your purchases. It might be from an institution (like a bank) or an individual (like a parent or carer).

In the finance world, you are constantly having to balance your assets (anything of value that you own) and your liabilities (anything you owe) to make sure that you are never in a position in which you owe more than you own.

This balancing act is an important part of adult life. As your earnings and money-management ability grow, underpinned by your Royal Money Mindset of course, you will develop your own strategies for making sure your assets grow and your liabilities shrink.

When this is reversed and you end up owing more than you own, then you could potentially find yourself on the brink of financial catastrophe—otherwise known as bankruptcy. In this situation, you might be unable to pay what you owe to your lenders, even if you sell everything you own, and as a result are legally classified as bankrupt, which could impact future employment and access to banking services.

I'm not telling you this to frighten you, but to remind you that the thing about putting on our crowns is that sometimes those crowns get heavy. But by arming ourselves with as much knowledge as possible in advance, we can put ourselves in the best position to avoid some of life's pitfalls, financial or not.

Let's check out some of the most common types of debt you should be familiar with.

1. Credit cards

"Do you take credit cards?"

"No problem, just charge it to the card."

"OMG I've maxed out my credit card!"

Do any of these sound familiar? They're lines that we hear time and again in TV shows or movies. In fact, these statements are so commonplace that they've become embedded in our daily discourse as completely normal. For most of us, we wouldn't even raise an eyebrow. But I really need you to. Starting today. Why?

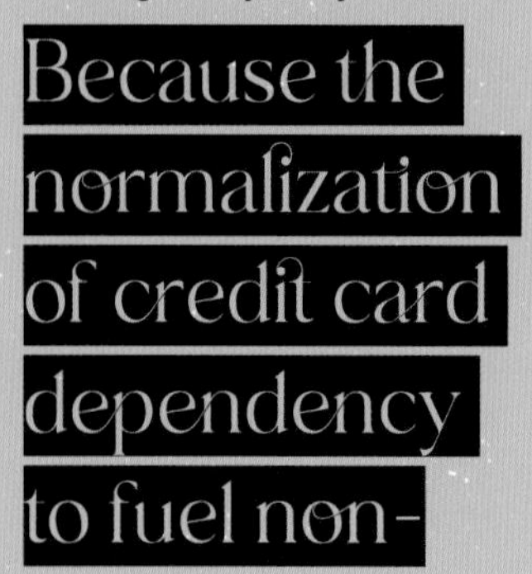

Because the normalization of credit card dependency to fuel non-essential spending is a path to losing control of your financial habits completely.

Credit cards work by giving you a cash boost that you can use anytime, anywhere. For some, it provides an extension of your income, enabling you to spend beyond what your earnings allow. In exchange for this, credit card providers will charge you interest, although unlike the interest rates you're likely to generate on a cash savings account, the interest you pay on your credit card debt is likely to be significantly higher.

Why you need to exercise caution

• Credit card debt is known as "revolving credit" because it has no fixed pay-off date and instead remains available to you as long as you continue to use it, paying off at least the minimum due. This potentially creates a life-long dependency that you will have difficulty shaking, undermining your ability to budget and live within your means.

• You are rewarded with more credit, the more you use it. This is a red flag. Our aim is to reduce our debt, not increase it.

LET'S TALK ABOUT CREDIT

You might be wondering how debt providers such as banks know whether you'd be a good person to offer credit to in the first place. After all, they need to feel quite confident that when they lend you money, you'll pay it back and not run away! One of the main ways they do this is by looking at your credit score.

A WORD ON CREDIT SCORES

Your credit score is an appraisal of your "attractiveness" as a customer by lenders, specifically when it comes to offering you credit. With thousands of people applying for credit every day, it is a way of assessing everyone equally by giving them a score typically, but not always, out of 1,000. This is based on a standard set of criteria which include the following:

1) **Whether you're registered to vote:** not because they care which way you vote, but because it shows them that you have a fixed address that matches the address you put on your application. This gives lenders greater comfort that you are who you say you are and live where you say you live should they need to contact you.

2) **Other borrowings:** how much credit you've already been offered by other lenders will also be a factor in any decision. Either in terms of how much a lender will offer based on what you've already got, or whether they'll offer you anything at all.

3) **Repayment track record:** does your history show you've been good at making repayments or do you regularly miss payments?

4) **Credit utilization:** how much of the total credit available to you (i.e., your total credit limits combined) are you already using? For example, if you've got two credit cards offering you $600 in total and you've already used $500 of it, then that's a lending red flag.

This list is not exhaustive. But you get the idea. Think of your score like a grade. The higher it is, the better. Scoring an F when you need at least a B to get access to additional finance when you need it, could mean you hear "no" when you want to hear "yes." Or that the yes has more strings attached to it than you would like. If you ever hear people say they've ruined their credit, this is typically what they mean: when it comes to their ability to borrow money, they are not "A" students.

The quirky and unfortunate thing about credit scores is that the only way to build yours is to actually have some credit in the first place. It may not be something you need to worry about right now, but as you get older and plan to make more significant purchases, then you might want to finance them in part through debt.

Even if you don't have an immediate need for credit, having a good credit score is another signal of your financial health, alongside some of the factors we've already discussed which include budgeting, saving, and investing for future you.

Here are some of the other types of debt you should know.

2. Loans

A loan operates in a similar way to a credit card; however, the key difference is that a loan is typically taken over a longer timeframe, has a fixed end date, and fixed repayment amounts. You might take a loan spread across five years, with a specific rate of interest that does not change for the length of time you have the loan, paid off in equal instalments every month. This is what is known as a personal loan.

SPECIAL PURPOSE LOANS

STUDENT LOAN

A loan that is typically offered by government-backed or private financial institutions to finance your higher education, typically at college level.

MORTGAGE

A loan secured against a property. A mortgage is usually the longest-term loan you will have with an average lifespan of 20–30 years. Unlike most other loans, if you fail to keep up your mortgage repayments, your mortgage provider has the right to reclaim the property, sell it, and recoup the money they would otherwise have lost. *Gulp*.

3. Overdraft

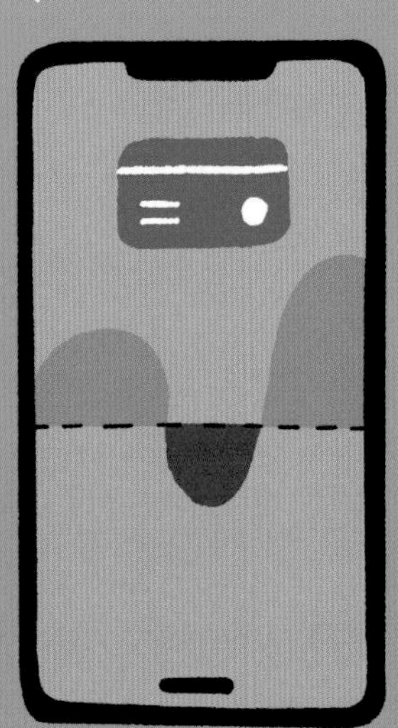

An overdraft is a source of debt that is attached to your bank account, essentially extending your income by allowing you to spend more than you earn in the event of an emergency. They are intended to be used on a short-term basis and settled relatively quickly and so are usually expensive, with high interest rates.

An overdraft is often most people's first introduction to debt. Some accounts are set up with an overdraft option already in place. If you don't need it, have this option removed straightaway. And if you do use it, make sure you settle it asap.

One trap that many people fall into is thinking that it's *their* money because you can so easily use it from your main bank account. This is false. An overdraft is debt, just like any other, and should be treated with caution.

4. BNPL

Speaking of caution, let's talk about Buy Now Pay Later. This kind of debt has been around for ages but the new wave of BNPL looks a little glossier these days. A little more… tempting. Quite often attached to beautiful images of the latest clothes and shoes, it has become the fastest growing way to get credit quickly with just a few clicks on your cell phone, enabling you to buy from some retailers without worrying about whether you have the money to pay straightaway.

Instead, you are invited to load up your shopping cart knowing that you won't have to pay it off for a few weeks. Sounds good, doesn't it? Well, not exactly. Because this kind of thinking undermines everything we've covered so far, from deferred gratification to budgeting, and as a result can be a slippery slope to losing control of your spending. Anything that looks too good to be true, usually is.

That's a lot of information to take in so here's a quick summary:

Credit type	Time span	Payment type	Purpose
Credit cards	Indefinite/ revolving	Non-fixed	General
Loans – Personal – Mortgage – Student	Medium to long term (5+ years)	Fixed	General House Education
Overdraft	Indefinite/ revolving	Non-fixed	General
BNPL	Short term (< 1 year)	Non-fixed	Consumer goods, fashion

IS IT EVER OK TO GET CREDIT?

As you've probably already gathered, uncontrolled debt use is not the best way to keep your finances in check, particularly when your purpose for getting it is for things you could easily acquire yourself with a little discipline and some saving. Here are some examples of when debt might and might not be OK.

WHEN IS DEBT OK?

When it's used to invest in an asset that could potentially be worth more in future. Think home ownership, or your education. Both of these have the potential to generate more money for you in the future and on this basis are good strategic reasons for extending the money you already have by borrowing some to enhance it.

When it's used to finance needs and not wants. For some of us, already on a strict budget, a sudden and unexpected rise in our cost of living could add to our financial fragility. Short-term borrowing until we figure out a long-term plan to deal with these added costs could provide a lifeline and ultimately peace of mind.

WHEN IS DEBT NOT OK?

When it's used to buy a rapidly depreciating (declining in value) asset like a car when it is not essential to your daily life (for example to get you to work or college), and you already have the savings to buy a cheaper one in cash.

To buy another black dress on BNPL when you already have five identical ones in your wardrobe, because *this* one has a gold zip that changes everything. (It really doesn't).

If after reading this, you do find yourself taking debt in future, here are five ways to make sure you stay firmly in the driving seat:

1) Pay it off regularly and ***set a clear target*** for settling the balance. Don't let it go on indefinitely with no fixed end date.

2) Try to pay ***more than the minimum amount you owe***. Doing this will help prevent your total borrowing costs, once interest is added, from spiralling.

3) Use it only for a specific purpose, having exhausted all other avenues. ***Think last, not first, resort.***

4) Use a comparison site and ***go for the lowest rates*** available.

5) ***Keep your credit limit low.*** There's no need for the total amount of money you could potentially borrow to keep creeping up. Always remember, things like this are in the debt provider's favor, not yours, which is why they will continually offer you more money seemingly as a reward for "good behavior" aka paying your debt off on time.

Stay alert: your mission is to keep your borrowings low and manageable.

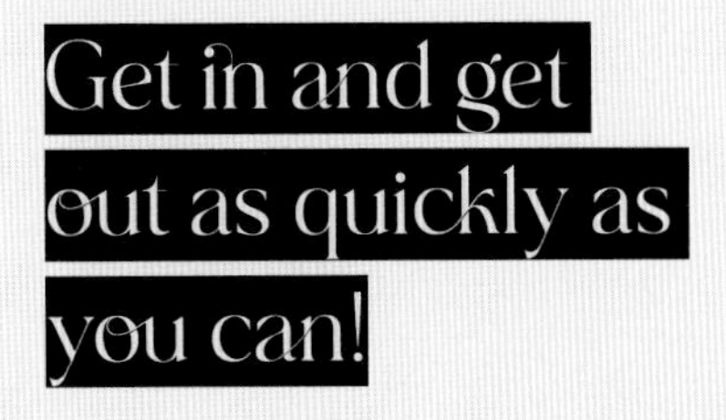

HERE ARE THREE SIMPLE SWAPS YOU CAN MAKE TO KEEP YOUR DEBT USAGE TO A MINIMUM

- Swap BNPL for a rental service. If fashion is your first love, do it sustainably and borrow the latest styles instead of buying them.

- Swap a personal loan to buy a car for saving. Remember your budget from before? Set up a new pot for a car and watch it grow as you put your money-management skills to good use.

- Swap your overdraft for more precise budgeting so you spend only what you make.

Quiz

So back to that outfit for your birthday. Knowing what you know now about debt, healthy spending habits, and retaining control, what's your next logical step?

a) Trust your seamstress to make an outfit in your size, according to your precise measurements, with a fabric within your budget. You'll look amazing whatever you wear so you want to feel comfortable and not go broke in the process!

b) Not bother to go to the party—if you can't have what you want what's the point?

c) Blow the budget and get the fabric you want even though it's more than you can afford. Go hard or go home!

If you chose **a**, then your Royal Money Mindset is strong. Well done, keep going!

If you chose **b**, then the phrase, "pitching a tantrum" springs to mind. Remember who you are and resist the urge to throw a tantrum. It's not a good look.

And if you chose **c**... No. Just, no. Go back to the beginning of this chapter and think about your choices again!

CROWN JEWELS

So now you have an understanding of some of the different types of debt, common pitfalls to avoid, and how to ensure that any debt use is fit for purpose.

Here are three key things to remember:

1. Cut your cloth according to your size or, in other words, spend only what you earn after savings, bills, and other commitments. Treat debt as a last resort for essential spending only.

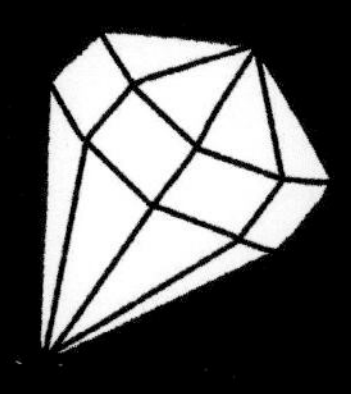

2. Your credit score is just one gauge of your financial health and is used by lenders such as banks to decide whether or not to lend you money.

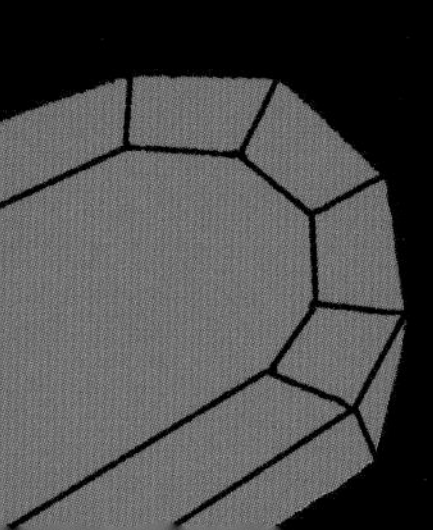

3. There are instances where debt use can make sense, such as to invest in assets like your education or property, which grow in value over time. Assess each situation on its own merits.

CHAPTER EIGHT

THE FREEDOM FUND

Hopefully by this stage in the book you're feeling quite confident in your ability to conquer these steps with ease. These fundamental building blocks to managing your money will go a long way to helping you set solid foundations for your future.

But the thing about money is that it is about more than just the practicality of how much you make, how much you spend, and how much you save. Yes, all of this is important too. But do you want to know one of the best things that money can bring...
The freedom to dream.

The freedom to dream

Or even, to imagine a life *beyond* our wildest dreams. This is where we can have some fun. Before we go on, let's look at an important life lesson.

Depending on who you're surrounded by and the kinds of media you consume, spanning everything from social media, TV podcasts, and blogs, your perspective on the relationship between money and your level of happiness will differ.

If all you see on social media, for example, are people posing in luxurious surroundings, holding wads of cash while seemingly living glamorous lifestyles, you might be led to believe that these things are essential ingredients in your quest for happiness too.

I'm here to tell you, nothing could be further from the truth.

If you were hanging a painting in your room, for example, the hammer that you use to knock in the nail that the painting will hang from is an important tool in the process purely for its ability to help us get from point A to point B efficiently and fuss-free. But do we care about the hammer itself? How big or small it is? Whether the handle is gold-plated? No. We care about the painting. And more importantly, the feelings of happiness that it conjures up whenever we look at it.

The same principle applies when it comes to your money. Use your hammer in the wrong way and you bash your finger. Using your money unwisely could bring similar misery.

But when you're clear on how you intend to use the tool you've been given, whether it's a hammer or your cash, and what you hope to achieve as a result, your likelihood of success is much higher.

But first things first, what exactly is a **freedom fund?** Good question. Look at it this way: if your rainy-day fund is destined to help you dig yourself out of a ditch quickly in the event that something comes up you hadn't planned for, then your freedom fund should be used to help you live your dream life. To literally free yourself from situations that might be stifling you or preventing you from being your very best self.

This could vary depending on the circumstance:

• Maybe you're in a job that, despite your best efforts, isn't moving you in the direction of your dream career and you're ready to make the leap to something new.

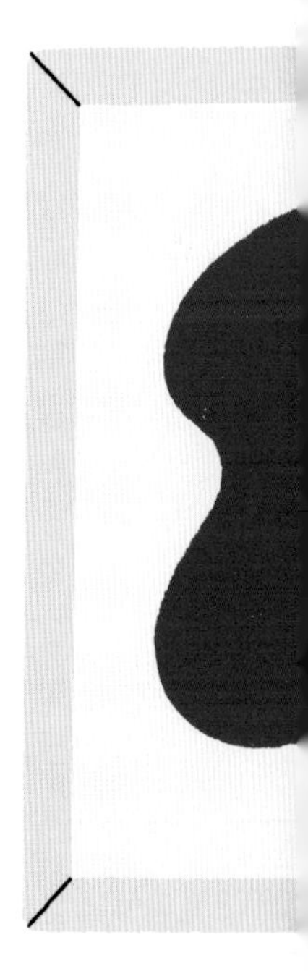

• Perhaps you want to live and work abroad for a year.

• Or freedom for you could mean going back to study as an adult, purely for the love of learning (sidenote: if you're knee deep in exams at the time of reading this, then you may laugh out loud at this idea, but it is definitely possible!).

Whatever the situation, it is likely that money will play a role in helping you get there.

ACTIVITY

What do you think you might use your freedom fund for? Write down some of the characteristics of your dream life. For example, where you might live, what experiences you'd like to have, or how you might spend your days.

Now get creative! Grab some magazines, glue, scissors, a large piece of paper or cardboard if you have some, and create a collage of your dream life. Cut out pictures and words that represent the dream life you've written down. The end result is known as your vision board. A single snapshot of the grand plans you have for your life.

Put your completed board somewhere you'll see it every day. This will motivate and inspire you to stay focused on what you plan to do next. Why not create a vision board party with your friends and invite everyone to look towards the future with you.

Pro tip: this is not the time to be shy about your dreams—take the handbrake off and really go for it. Your vision board should be the embodiment of future you—feel free to give it a name if that helps!

Let's get SMART

How did that exercise feel? Hopefully you're feeling super pumped and excited about your future plans. With your potential there are no limits to what you can achieve, but sometimes we have to give our imaginations a good stretch in order to conceive of what this reality could be.

Now we need to organize these dreams into individual goals. The framework we'll use for this is SMART. You might be wondering why we need to do this in the first place. After all, you've just done a mega brain dump of everything you've earmarked your freedom fund for. Surely that's it?

Well, not quite. Here are three reasons why breaking down your goals is so important.

- **Clarity**

Your vision board is intended to be a beautiful tapestry of your future dream life. Think of it like one of those kaleidoscopes you might have played with as a child, that changes every time you turn it. A riot of color and imagination with no particular order to it, just free flowing hopes and dreams. Your goals are a way to help you get crystal clear on what these hopes are and to pinpoint precisely what you are hoping to achieve.

- **Discipline**

Discipline has come up a few times in this book, hasn't it? I hope you don't switch off when you see it, but instead recognize its power in helping you to stay the course so your dreams don't remain just that: dreams. Your discipline is one of the essential ingredients that will help you bring them to reality.

- **Focus**

You know that blurry-eyed feeling you have when you first wake up in the morning? Well, this is the opposite. And it should hopefully give you a perfect example of why laser focus is so important in achieving our goals. Just as it would probably be unwise to leap straight out of bed before you rub your eyes first to avoid crashing into a wall, moving at pace towards your dream life in an uncoordinated way could potentially have an equally unsuccessful, and painful, outcome.

A simple way to remember how to organize your goals in a way that helps you achieve the above, is to think SMART. SMART is a commonly used framework that prompts you to make sure your goals are:

Specific: what exactly are you trying to achieve? If your vision board was the sketch, this is where you color it in. Be precise!

Measurable: how will you know if you've succeeded?

Achievable: is what you're aiming for a real possibility for you? Or are you setting such lofty goals e.g., plucking a star from the sky on your next night flight, that you will never be able to reach them? If you are, then you may well be self-sabotaging. Don't be afraid to course-correct if you need to.

Realistic: is now a good time or should you wait? Don't allow yourself or others to sabotage your dreams by telling you they're out of reach, but equally you'll need to judge whether your "now" might need to be a "not yet."

Timebound: how likely are you to do it if there's no deadline? Apply a little urgency and give yourself a date to work towards.

Let's say one of the ambitions that you've stuck on to your vision board is to spend six months traveling through Africa. Here's how you might apply SMART.

SPECIFIC	To travel to three countries in West Africa, spending two months in each: Ghana, Togo, and Cote D'Ivoire.
MEASURABLE	I will measure this in passport stamps!
ACHIEVABLE	I will focus specifically on certain countries recognizing Africa is a massive continent and I cannot cover it completely in six months.
REALISTIC	I have selected those countries that are safe for me to visit to as a solo traveler or as part of an organized group.
TIMEBOUND	To be achieved on or before x date or x birthday.

So, now having established one of the goals from our dream life, we need to calculate the cost of achieving it.

Are you willing to pay the price?

But what are the different costs associated with achieving our goals? There are four main costs we will consider here:

1) Financial: What is the tangible, monetary cost?

2) Emotional: How will you feel about achieving this goal? Happy? Sad? Indifferent? Pay close attention to this. We want to feel enriched, inspired, and uplifted, not deflated.

3) Mental: What mental capacity do you have to pursue this goal right now? Is it likely to cause an unhealthy amount of stress or is the level of pressure manageable?

4) Opportunity: What do you stand to gain or lose from choosing your preferred option over the others that exist?

Let's work through the above example.

COST	EXAMPLE IN PRACTICE
Financial	Flights, accommodation, food, travel insurance, entertainment, etc.
Mental	How much bureaucracy and red tape will be involved in planning this trip? What additional vaccinations will I need? (e.g., yellow fever). Will the many hoops I will need to jump through tip me over the edge and cause me unmanageable stress or is this a good learning opportunity I can cope with and will benefit from?
Emotional	Will I be too homesick being away from home for that length of time? Who might I miss and how much? Will I be able to cope, or will I be desperately unhappy?
Opportunity	If I go traveling for six months, will I miss out on the internship at that law firm I like or if they made me an offer, would they allow me to defer it for a year on the basis that the experience the trip will afford me is invaluable?

ACTIVITY

Now pick a goal from your vision board and apply the four-cost test from the previous pages. Give each cost category a score from 1-5 where 1 is "unaffordable" and 5 "affordable." If your total score is 8 or below—treat that as reflection that perhaps the cost is currently too great to bear. If you scored 16 and above in total—this could mean that you're ready to go. Anything in between is a question mark and should be examined more closely before you reach a conclusion

CAUTION

These scores should be used as a guide only. Scoring highly in some categories but poorly in others, could artificially inflate your results and mean that your definitive "yes" might be a "not yet" and conversely your definitive "no" might be a "maybe."

Use your own good judgment and proceed wisely.

Now you've examined all the costs, the big question is, can you afford it?

It's a nerve-wracking thought, isn't it? But that's the thing about the Royal Money Mindset, it's not all freedom fund planning and fun. It's also about facing up to the responsibilities placed on our shoulders by the wealth of knowledge and resources we have at our fingertips. Suddenly, saying we don't know just isn't an option. We do and if not, we will.

Applying these frameworks to your dream goals is not intended to deter you. Quite the opposite in fact. This is your chance to whip them in order. To prioritize them and decide which ones you want to pursue first, which ones you want to park for later and which ones you've decided on reflection you want to abandon completely.

And let me let you in on a little secret: there is no shame at all in deciding that having assessed all the costs, it's just too expensive. This may mean you decide to wait until you can afford the associated costs or, at the most extreme end of the spectrum, that they're just too costly for you full stop.

And that's OK.

What isn't OK is allowing yourself to drift aimlessly, with no clear direction, visualizing a wonderful life but never doing anything about it beyond daydreaming, and even worse never giving yourself the credit for being a total boss who can do amazing things if you just put your mind to it.

So big girl panties on and ask yourself these critical questions:

1) Can you afford it?
2) What steps might you take to be able to afford it?
3) Are you willing to pay the price?

The answers could be truly life-changing.

CROWN JEWELS

Freedom fund planning and visualization can be a super fun way of getting excited about the future. But the best way to put yourself in the driving seat, is to work through a system that can help you filter what truly matters to you, what it costs, and whether you have what it takes to get there (spoiler alert, you do). Here's a recap of the key things to remember.

1.

Your freedom fund is a pot of money you start building, in a completely separate stash to your rainy-day fund for emergencies, to help you live your dream life.

2.

Visualization is a great starting point for thinking about your dream life. Think big and use your imagination, then capture it on a vision board to keep you motivated.

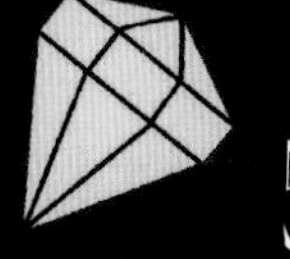

3.

When it comes to your goals, just remember, think SMART (Specific, Measurable, Achievable, Realistic and Timebound).

4.

There are four main costs associated with achieving your goals. Calculating this cost will help you decide whether it's a "yes," "no," or "not yet."

5.

Choosing to abandon certain goals having assessed all the costs is not an admission of defeat. Just savvy goal planning and ruthless prioritization. Exactly what you'd expect from someone with a Royal Money Mindset.

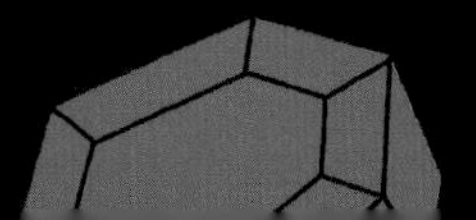

CHAPTER NINE

YOUR MONEY TRIBE MATTERS

Have you ever heard the expression, "you're known by the company you keep?" Or "choose your friends wisely?" To avoid any kind confusion, this relates to more than just picking cool friends.

In fact, the social currency of your friends is the least of your worries here. Instead, whenever the people in your life offer this very wise advice, they're encouraging you to reflect more on the character of the individuals in your social circle.

Who are they as people? What are some of their best and worst personality traits?

What are their aspirations? Do they have big plans for their lives, or have they shrunk their ambitions down?

How do they treat others? Are they kind or unkind? Toxic or supportive?

How do they treat themselves? Do they speak positively about themselves and forgive themselves for mistakes?

You might be wondering, what's this got to do with our cash? Surely our relationship with money is personal and should be managed completely separately from our friendships.

The truth is, when it comes to our money, or any other aspect of our lives for that matter, the people we surround ourselves with really counts.

Here's why:

1. In the words of motivational speaker Jim Rohn,

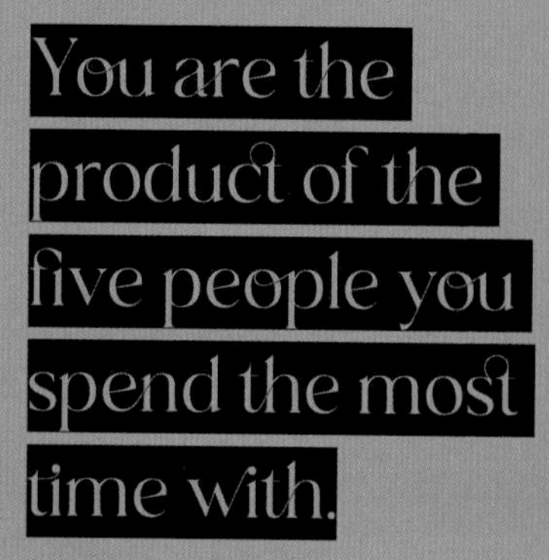

Which means even if you're not aware of it, the people around you are definitely rubbing off on you.

2. Our friends play more than just a social role in our lives as sources of entertainment and leisure. What about when we need a motivational boost, a shoulder to cry on, or help solving a problem?

It's often in times of crisis that we really realize who our friends are.

Considering this in advance means that you will always have a solid team to lift you up you when you're unable to help yourself.

3. Ever heard the expression,

You never get a second chance to make a first impression.

Well, this applies as much to the people we spend our time with as it does the impression we make as individuals.

Does your social circle have a positive reputation or a negative one and, most importantly, is this a fair assessment? Only you can make this judgment. But be aware, whether you like it or not, judgments are definitely being made.

ACTIVITY

Outside of your family, who are the five people you spend most of your time with? Assuming you are a mix of all five people, would you be satisfied with the result? Why or why not?

You may remember in chapter one, we introduced the concept of money scripts, or those behaviors linked to how we manage our money that we inherit from the people that raise us. We looked at those scripts through the eyes of four different girls, each with a different relationship with money.

Our money tribes take this idea a step further. Imagine that the world is made up of billions of people from all walks of life, with different backgrounds experiences and upbringings. Those same people are then thrown together in schools, jobs, sports clubs, and other social settings where they become friends.

A new tribe is formed.

But what exactly is a tribe?

In anthropological terms, a tribe is a group of people linked by social, economic, religious, or blood ties. Perhaps your friendship group was formed because you have fun together playing hockey every week. Maybe you're in the same Spanish class. Or it could be that your friendship is based on history—you've all been friends since you were toddlers.

But when it comes to your cash, it doesn't automatically follow that all members of your squad are like-minded. Let's take a look at the following line-up.

Petty ("Petunia") Boop

Petty is constantly keeping score, whether it's to do with your love life, exam results, who ate the last slice of pizza at the sleepover, and who still owes her 50¢ from that time you caught the bus and one of you was a bit short. Yep, she's Petty alright. But you love her, nonetheless.

IMPACT ON YOU

The GOOD news

Petty keeps you on your toes. She forces you to be accountable for your money moves and to reduce financial dependence on others—however big or small.

The BAD news

Spending too much time around people like this could raise your anxiety levels unnecessarily as you constantly worry about being critiqued.

Moderate Meena

Moderate Meena is the peacemaker of the group. She's able to see things from all perspectives, doesn't take sides, and can always be relied upon to give a balanced view. Everything in moderation. She cuts her cloth according to her size, spends her money on the things she loves, but knows when to save too. Her calm, considered wisdom has been a real game-changer in helping you level up your budgeting skills this year.

IMPACT ON YOU

The GOOD news

Moderate Meena has really helped you view life from a different perspective. Nothing is done in extremes, she plans for all eventualities, but also makes space for fun. Meena lives by the mantra "fail to plan, plan to fail" and as a result of your friendship with her, you've been able to see first-hand the benefits that come with this approach, for all things including your money. Meena is also completely unafraid to discuss money openly, which is super refreshing and has massively helped to increase your financial confidence.

The BAD news

With Meena, when it comes to your money, there really isn't any downside. After all, what could be wrong with considering all the variables before you make a decision about where and when to part with your hard-earned cash? Just make sure that you don't spend too long weighing up all the options before you take your next step. While patience is a virtue, sometimes a little pace can help you to pounce on the best opportunities before it's too late.

Careful Clara

Like Meena, Clara is another money-management queen, but her brand of budgeting comes with a hefty dose of nervous energy. She's anxious about over-spending, is worried about never having enough, and generally prefers to err on the side of caution, whatever she is doing. Clara's idea of risk is choosing a cheeseburger over her usual chicken burger and the idea of the unknown terrifies her. That said, she is fiercely self-reliant and takes her financial independence seriously, which is something you really admire.

IMPACT ON YOU

The GOOD news

The thing about Clara is that, despite seeming as though she is constantly on edge whenever the topic of money comes up, Clara's ability to guard her financial independence at all costs is inspiring. She's opened your eyes to a new world of financial feminism in which young women, just like you, put themselves in the driving seat when it comes to their cash and leave nothing to chance.

The BAD news

Unfortunately, despite all that care and attention Clara pays to her money, her obsessive approach sucks all the joy out of life. Yes, there are certainly lessons you can learn from Clara about pinching your pennies, but we must also remember that one of the greatest benefits of financial discipline and control is the freedom it gives us to enjoy the things that make us smile.

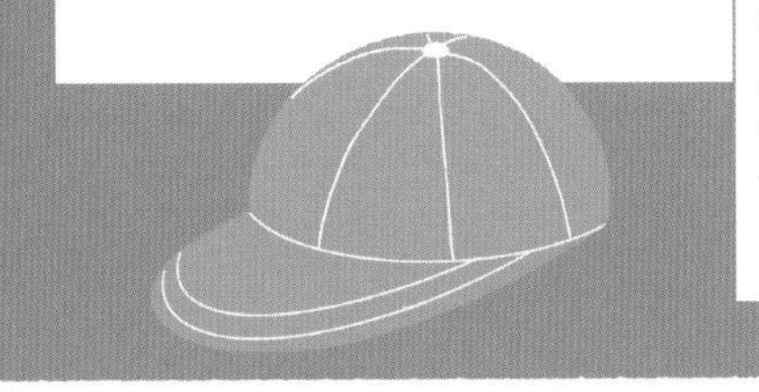

Debbie Downer

Debbie can be a real vibe killer at times. She doesn't mean to be, but she can always see the downside, whatever the circumstances. Tell her you want to study at a particular college and she'll tell you not to get your hopes up because it's so hard to get in to. Remind her of the plans you'd made to do a gap year after sixth form and she'll bring up the number of people who've been kidnapped on that route and, by the way, how are you ever going to afford it with just *that* Saturday job? It's exhausting and seemingly never-ending.

IMPACT ON YOU

The GOOD news

Well, if you ever need a reality check you can count on Debbie to give you one. She's not going to sugar coat it or lull you into a false sense of security and, actually, there are times when we all need that.

The BAD news

This is one personality type that needs to be approached with caution. There is nothing worse than being in the company of someone who sucks the oxygen out of the room with one big sigh. Who is constantly reminding you to lower your expectations and ambitions and who makes you feel quite hopeless. Too long around Debbie and you'll abandon your dreams and resign yourself to a life of mediocrity. If there's one person whose Royal Money Mindset needs a tune-up, it's Debbie.

Flashy Felicia

Flashy Felicia is the live wire of the group. There's never a dull moment when she's around. Felicia loves nothing more than being the centre of attention and will happily spend every penny she has to make that happen. She has expensive tastes and is a real thrillseeker. She's the one in your group who always knows what's trending from a style perspective and is constantly on the hunt for the perfect Instagrammable image, however detached from reality this may be.

IMPACT ON YOU

The GOOD news

Felicia is great fun. She's the party starter, vibe giver, permanent adventure hunter. She reminds you to squeeze all the juice out of life and to really live for today. Energy that we could all do with from time to time.

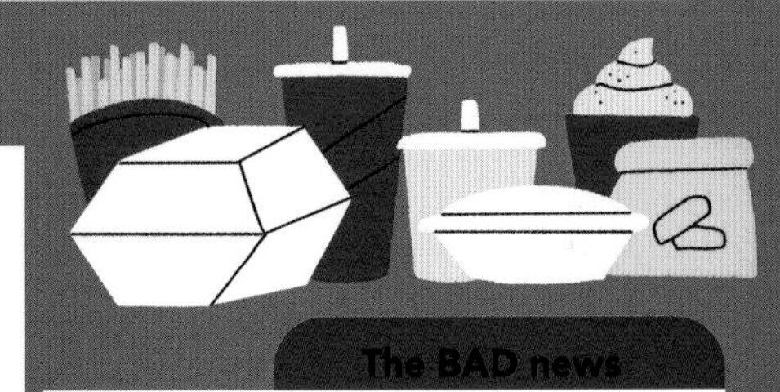

The BAD news

The trouble is, spending time with Felicia quite often has a hefty price tag attached to it. Shopping trips for one specific item become sprees, birthday lunches become dinners and bowling, even a medium-sized McDonald's becomes super-sized. She does nothing by halves and that's not always good for your bank balance—especially when she's borrowing from you!

Do you recognize any of these characters in your friendship group?

Of course, there are many other personality types that might be on display among our group of friends. This isn't an exhaustive list by any means. It's also fair to say that sometimes we cycle through multiple personalities at different points in our lives depending on the circumstances or even just on the day. But it's important to be attuned to the ways the people around us influence our thoughts, habits, and behaviors because it could be the difference between achieving the financial goals we set ourselves and not.

So, what exactly should you be looking out for?

Toxic money behaviors to avoid

1. OBSESSIVE BUDGETING WITH NO CLEAR GOAL IN SIGHT

It's fine to be careful with your money, but not to the point of misery. Spending too much time around these people could give you anxiety for no good reason. Focus on setting solid foundations by applying the principles in this book and using money as a tool to help you achieve what you want to. Not a threat to be approached with caution.

2. OVER-SPENDING WITHOUT THINKING ABOUT THE FUTURE

Be wary of those people who might influence you to spend beyond your means and to forget the future entirely. A little balance goes a long way.

3. BECOMING A VICTIM OF "LIFESTYLE CREEP"

That is, being influenced by others to live a life that you cannot afford. Remember that what you might see from the outside looking in, whether it's on social media or people that you admire in real life, may not actually be reality. Anybody can take a good picture after all. Focus on living a life true to you, which is aligned to the goals you've set for yourself—nobody else.

4. ADOPTING A SCARCITY MINDSET

Or, in other words, the belief that you that you cannot change your financial future no matter what you do so why bother trying? There will occasionally be times when a setback can make us feel down in the dumps but being permanently mired in a state of hopelessness can be depressing for everyone around you.

5. BORROWING MONEY WITH NO PLAN TO PAY IT BACK

This is a big no-no. Falling out with friends over money just isn't worth it. If your friends trust you enough to lend you money in the first place, respect their trust and pay it back—on time!

Do you recognize any of these toxic money behaviors among your friends? Here's what you can do about it.

1. SET SOLID BOUNDARIES

The best friendships are those in which there is mutual respect for one another's differences (and similarities), including when it comes to money. Where you are pursuing different goals and perhaps have different money-management approaches, give one another the space to exercise those differences, while encouraging one another to be better where it makes sense to do so. This might mean reminding your bestie of her plan to go traveling at year end, which may mean that spending her planned saving on a new gadget is unwise. It might also mean that she understands that your plan to save for a state-of-the-art podcasting equipment so you can finally launch your new show is a complete non-negotiable and so won't twist your arm to come out at the weekend if it could put this plan in jeopardy.

2. LEAD BY EXAMPLE

You might be further along in your money-management journey than your friends, based on some of the learning you've done so far. You're probably buzzing with all the wonderful new ways you can save and spend, budget, and invest your money. Your friends, though, might be at a less advanced stage and have no idea where to even begin. This is a great opportunity for you to lead by example and become the go-to person for money tips and recommendations based on your trial and error. What a great position to be in!

3. CREATE AN ACCOUNTABILITY TEAM

Linked to the above, why not, as part of your newfound leadership, set a regular money date with your friends to talk all things money and hold one another to account. This might include how you're getting on with your savings, checking in on your goals, discussing the latest money apps to help you stay on track and generally cheerleading and supporting one another to financial success. This is a great discipline to maintain even as you get older—talking about money among the safety of people you know and trust is a power move.

4. DEMONSTRATE EMPATHY BUT KNOW WHEN TO LET GO

Nobody's saying that having a Royal Money Mindset is about making the perfect money moves at all times. We're people after all, not robots. That means, while we should be open to learning and improving as well as sharing our skills with others, cheerleading when required and making suggestions when required too, sometimes we might have to accept that with the best will in the world some people just aren't going to be ready to change. And that's OK. Your job is to be the best you can be, support your friends as much as you can, and learn when to let go. It doesn't mean you have to ditch your friends over it—while their money personality might be a bit off-key, the rest of your relationship may be super rewarding. It is only when the entire relationship becomes toxic and affects you in other aspects of your life, too, that you might want to review whether your BFF has become a frenemy.

INSIGHT

In studies, women are often shown as being reluctant or embarrassed to talk about money with their peers. And this costs us greatly from salary negotiations (where we're afraid to ask for more money, even if it is available) to investment decisions (where we're shown to favor cash over the stock market). Put your Royal Money Mindset to good use and lead the conversation among your friends. You'll be setting yourself up for a lifetime of openness around money as a result, which is a wonderful thing.

CROWN JEWELS

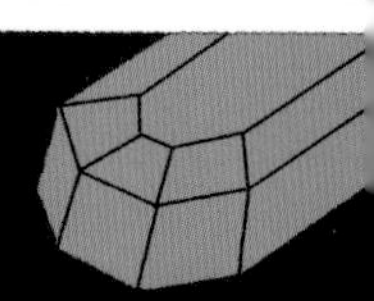

Did you know how important your friends were to your bank balance? Well, if you didn't, here's a recap.

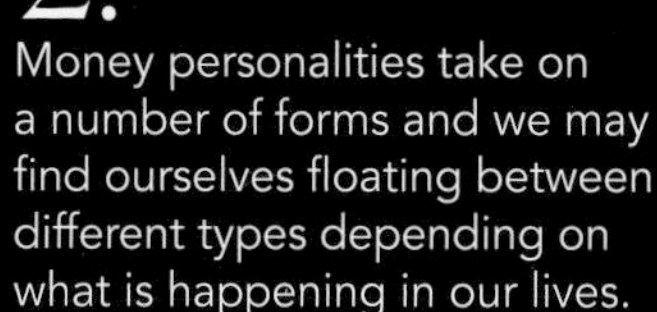

1. We are all the product of the five closest people to us—choose yours wisely.

2. Money personalities take on a number of forms and we may find ourselves floating between different types depending on what is happening in our lives.

3. Toxic money behaviors among our friends can derail us from achieving our goals if we let them. Set solid boundaries about money so your friends know what you will and will not tolerate and don't be afraid to issue a red flag if your wishes are not being recognized. Mutual respect is key.

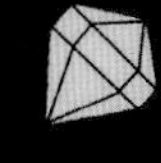

4. Don't be afraid to lead by example—not everyone will know what you know so don't judge. Find ways to show what good money management looks like and be willing to learn from others too.

5. Create an accountability group with your friends to stay on track.

CHAPTER TEN

IF IT LOOKS TOO GOOD TO BE TRUE, IT PROBABLY IS

Imagine the following scene. You've received some good news so decide to stop by your favorite pancake place to celebrate, the one you've been going to for years. The lady who runs it, Marie, is French and has introduced you to the delights of a delicious traditional crêpe. You like yours done simply with a squeeze of lemon and a dusting of sugar.

But one day, when you visit for your usual Saturday morning breakfast, you discover that Marie is no longer flipping crêpes and is instead trying to sell you Korean fried chicken. "How random" you think, but she is insistent that she is an expert and that you won't find better Korean fried chicken anywhere else in the world. Even Korea!

Your instincts are immediately on high alert. First of all, what on Earth has prompted this sudden shift to chicken from crêpes? Surely cupcakes would have been a more logical next step? Secondly, with the best will in the world and while you don't want to cast any doubt on Marie's abilities, you're just not convinced that her Korean fried chicken is going to be as good as what you might be able to get in downtown Seoul.

You love Marie, you really do, but you decide to pass. It's not April Fool's Day after all.

The big "cashfish"

The scene I've just described, while harmless in this particular case, is becoming increasingly common when it comes to hoodwinking people financially. Let's call it "cashfishing."

You may have heard of "catfishing." This is a term used to describe a situation in which people having connected online but, never having met or seen one another face to face, might be tricked into believing the person they are speaking to is actually someone else. Perhaps they have used a fake profile, given a fake name, even pretended they live or work somewhere they don't.

The realization that you have been speaking to someone who isn't who they claim to be can be shocking at best and devastating at worst. The feeling of violation that someone could have preyed on your good nature to defraud you, isn't a good one.

Sadly, the online arena has created the conditions for lots of scenarios just like this one to take place. Only this time, they're preying on our cash. You only have to switch on social media to be confronted with videos and posts from people claiming to be experts in one thing or another, and, most of the time, we have no real way of verifying that they are who they say they are.

With billions of eyeballs up for grabs, the unscrupulous among us have no problem whatsoever taking advantage. Let's take a look at five different forms "cashfishing" might take.

1) BEING ASKED TO HOLD MONEY ON SOMEONE ELSE'S BEHALF IN YOUR ACCOUNT AND THEN TRANSFER IT ELSEWHERE AT A LATER DATE.

One way that you may unwittingly find yourself in a compromising situation is when you are asked for a favor from someone you've been speaking to online. You may have been chattering for weeks or even months, struck up a good rapport, and now feel a sense of comfort and familiarity with this person. Without you realizing, they may have been asking you questions and pretending to be interested in your life but all the time they may have just been grooming you to a place of total relaxation where the usual defenses you place around yourself to protect you, might be down.

One day this new friend might ask if you could hold some money for them. Nothing major, just a few thousand pounds. You ask why and are told a story that seems to make sense. It's a large amount of money, they say, we don't want to pay bank charges. They'd rather save that cash and pay it to you as a thank you for helping. How thoughtful of them!

But most of these people can't put this money directly into their own bank accounts. Not straightaway. Usually, they already have a criminal record and so they are aware that the authorities might be watching their every move. But sometimes it's because they have such an in-depth knowledge of the banking system that they know the level of scrutiny they might be under if they were to attempt to deposit a massive amount of money into their account in one go. Instead they break it up into parcels and distribute it across a number of individuals, often young, often vulnerable, and get them to make these smaller deposits instead, in exchange for a cash incentive.

All you have to do is be willing to receive the cash and make the transfer. No big deal right? **WRONG**.

This is money laundering, a crime that in the US could see you serve up to twenty years behind bars as an adult. It's a crime for which ignorance is no defense.

Money laundering is a way for people who have come into money from criminal activity, selling drugs say, to attempt to "clean" or "launder" this cash by placing it into legitimate channels, such as bank accounts, so they are able to get access to it without alerting the authorities.

2) BEING ENCOURAGED TO INVEST IN A NEW GET-RICH-QUICK SCHEME THAT CAN DOUBLE YOUR MONEY

They've been sliding into your DMs for weeks. Tagging you in posts showcasing their incredibly flashy lifestyle. Designer bags, clothes, and shoes and all the latest gadgets. It all looks truly amazing. Remember Flashy Felicia from the previous chapter? This would be the life of her dreams and it could be yours too! You too could multiply your money to six figures or more by following a simple formula to financial success, "guaranteed" to offer you double digit returns.

The details are vague and yes, the testimonials of people they claim to have achieved similar success look a little… well… suspect, but they're just so convincing. Perhaps it's forex trading—a highly specialized area of finance that requires a certain set of skills and experience to get right. Or maybe it's a brand of cryptocurrency or some "celebrity endorsed NFT" that your research seems to bring up nothing about. Whatever it is, if it looks too good to be true then… you know the rest.

3) BEING ASKED TO SEND MONEY TO SOMEONE IN DISTRESS

It's a little old-school, but just because it's an old scam doesn't mean it's not a threat to you. Maybe you get an email from someone who claims to know you from schooldays and they want to alert you to the fact they're in danger, but insist you keep it under wraps. They tell you they've exhausted all other avenues, you're their only hope, and that they are in grave danger without your help. Maybe they share something with you about a past experience, something they could easily have gleaned from your public social media profiles, to put you at ease. Maybe it's just a small amount of money at first. They might even have set up a bogus "gofundme" page specifically for the purpose. There are no lengths that a scammer won't go to it seems.

4) IDENTITY THEFT

So much of our existence takes place online these days, doesn't it? We have apps for everything from food to fashion (and hopefully finance now too!) and spend hours trawling social media on our smartphones, which also now passes for a payment method. We're digital natives in the truest senses of the word. We've never known life to exist exclusively offline. As a result, the digital footprint we leave behind, the clues of our presence online, is huge. We share our names and birthdays, we tag ourselves into locations near where we live, we show up in our friends' feeds, too, and together these breadcrumbs give ready and waiting scammers everything they need to clone your identity or, in other words—pretend to be you with financially devastating consequences.

THIS LIST IS NOT COMPLETE, OF COURSE. EVERY DAY THERE ARE NEW AND INNOVATIVE WAYS SCAMMERS COME UP WITH TO TAKE WHAT IS NOT THEIRS. BE ALERT!

5) TEXT SCAMS

You know the one that seems to crop up every now and then, telling you to click here or there on a link in order to collect your parcel from the post office. You're just about to click it when you realize, "wait one minute—I didn't order anything!" Clicking the link may seem harmless at first, but you may then be asked for personal details that the scammers can use to complete a jigsaw about you and your financial accounts in order to empty them. These tend to spike at certain times of the year, Christmas, say, when our seasonal scammers know that the volume of orders and deliveries is likely to be high. Be vigilant.

ACTIVITY

Have you experienced any of these in the past? List some of the different ways you've successfully swerved a cashfish situation!

Protecting yourself from being cashfished online

NINE RED FLAGS TO AVOID

1) Beware of any situation, money related or otherwise, in which you are told not to tell anyone what is happening. Talk to your parents or another adult you trust immediately.

2) Never give your bank details for any reason.

3) Do not divulge any of your personal information to anyone you've just met, even if they seem to be confirming details about your life. Instead, raise the alarm.

4) Be mindful of the information you share on social media and make your accounts private. Don't live under a cloak of fear but do take the necessary precautions. Do not post your whereabouts the second you get there, do not share details of your birthday, address, or other information that could be used to clone your identity.

5) If someone new expresses a sudden interest in you and the relationship develops quickly, perhaps they start buying you gifts or offering you things you'd never be able to afford by yourself, they are likely to be grooming you so they can take advantage of you in future. Trust your instincts and get a second opinion from a grown-up you can trust. A parent, godmother, aunt, or uncle, anyone who will be able to help you figure out what their motive might be and can involve the appropriate authorities.

6) Don't invest in anything that is unregulated and which promises the Earth overnight. Investing is a long-term game, not a get-rich-quick scheme. Anything that tells you otherwise is dodgy.

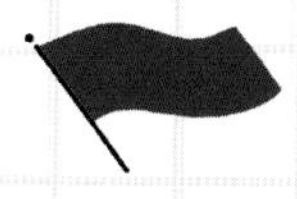

7) Avoid clicking on anything that looks suspicious. Malware risk, or viruses that could infect all of your devices, while stealing your passwords and other information, is real.

8) Pay for items online through an encrypted service like PayPal rather than with a debit card.

9) Be discerning about where you get your financial advice. TikTok and other platforms can be a great way to get bitesize chunks of information quickly but do check that the sources are credible and the information is accurate. Don't be seduced by glossy images or clever editing—focus solely on the quality of the message.

ACTIVITY

Do you follow any money accounts on social media? Which ones and why?

HERE ARE A COUPLE OF THINGS TO CHECK TO MAKE SURE THEY TRULY KNOW THEIR STUFF...

- Qualifications: what qualifies your finance favorites to talk about money management? Do they have practical personal experiences that you feel like you can relate to? Any finance qualifications? Or perhaps they've worked in the finance industry for a while. Whatever it is, make sure you get super comfortable that the people you choose to follow are worthy of your attention.

- Background and profile: are they who they say they are? Do a quick online search to check!

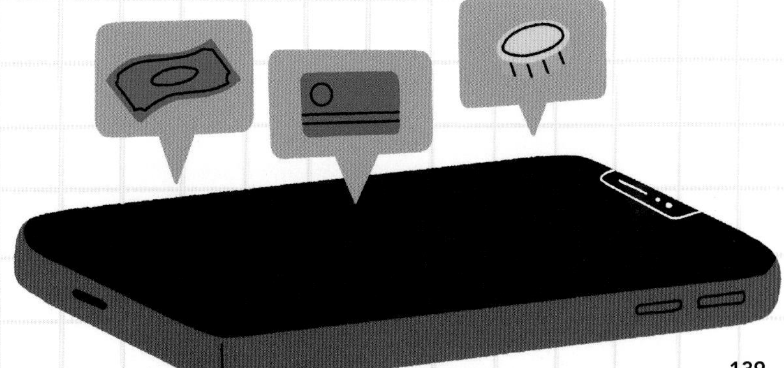

A word on financial abuse

But what about when the source of your financial distress is closer to home? And the people seeking to exploit the cracks in your protective armour are those you know and love? Financial abuse is a term used to describe any situation in which you feel threatened, intimidated, or forced by someone, usually close to you, to make financial decisions against your will and which could end up leaving you worse off.

WHAT ARE SOME CLUES?

• Perhaps you're forced to lend someone money when you don't want to.

• Maybe you're being bullied to take out credit cards in your name on someone else's behalf, forcing you into debt.

• It could be that someone controls how you spend your money or restricts access to the money you make, for example, by insisting that your earnings are paid into their bank account instead of your own.

Sadly, financial abuse is something that you or others you know might experience at some point in your life. Even worse, given it is linked to something that we guard so closely, our cash, it means that it is generally those closest to us that would be dishing out the abuse—from friends, to family members, to significant others.

They key thing to remember is that, in the unfortunate event that you go through this, it doesn't mean that you have done anything wrong, or that you have in some way caused it.

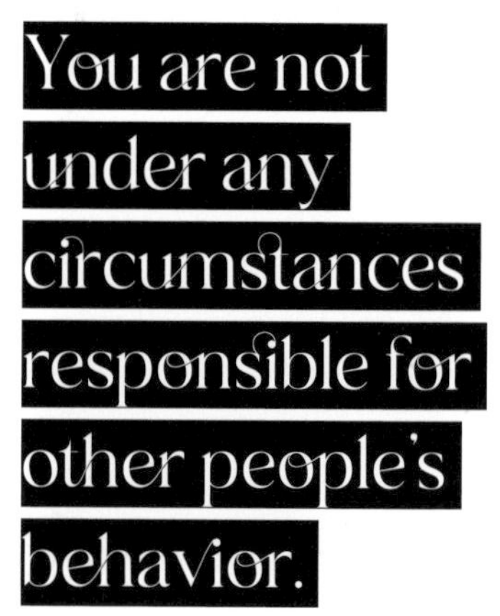

WHAT YOU CAN DO ABOUT IT

• Confide in someone you trust.
• Consider your circle carefully and stay attuned to any red flags early.
• Identify professional services you can contact anonymously where you live, to raise the alarm and receive guidance and support.

PLEASE DON'T

- Suffer alone or in silence.
- Blame yourself.
- Forget your magic—you are not defined by negative experiences.

SPOILER ALERT
Love does not show up as control, manipulation, or poor treatment of others. If this is what you are being told but your instincts are screaming otherwise: trust them. They are a crucial part of your Royal Money Mindset.

CROWN JEWELS

We've covered some important issues in this chapter, so it probably feels quite heavy. Here's a reminder of the main points to remember.

1. Social media can be a great way to get access to useful content, inspiration, and information on a whole host of topics, including money. Use your judgment to decide who deserves your attention—treat it as the jewel that it is.

2. Financial abuse involves being controlled by someone often close to you (but not always) around how to manage and access your money.

3. Many of us will know someone who's experienced or will personally experience financial abuse in our lifetimes. Look out for the clues and confide in someone you trust who can help you take the first step.

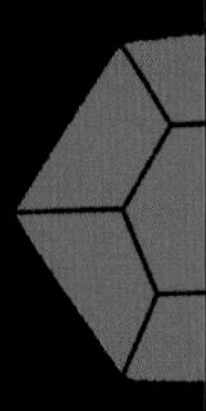

4. Avoid cashfishing! If something seems too good to be true, it is.

5. If you are the victim of a social-media scam or financial abuse, recognize that you are just that, a victim of a crime. It is neither your fault, nor are you to blame.

CHAPTER ELEVEN

PLANNING FOR TOMORROW, TODAY

Let's take a walk down memory lane, shall we, and cast our minds all the way back to chapter three, when we discussed the idea of **gratification.**

When we first covered it, (remember the marshmallows? Turn to page 32 if you need a quick refresher) it probably seemed a little detached from some of the other money lessons. A bit of an odd one out.

But what I hope you've gathered over the chapters that followed and now, as you will soon see, from this one too, is that

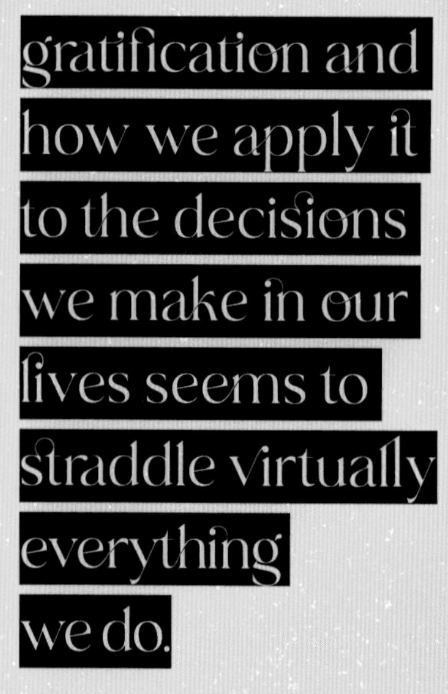

• Whether to save for a rainy day or blow the budget on a holiday because YOLO! (you only live once).

• Whether to follow Flashy Felicia's example and buy all the fast fashion expertly modeled by your favorite influencers (many of whom do not pay for the clothes and shoes they encourage you to buy) on a Buy Now Pay Later scheme because who's got time to wait until pay day?

• Whether you find yourself succumbing to the charms of a social media scammer, preying on your cash by promising you overnight riches.

It all adds up to the same thing: **using your judgment to make a decision that is best aligned to your goals.**

So now we're going to take a look at the ultimate deferral of gratification when it comes to our cash. The cherry on our well-iced cake. It's retirement planning. But first things first, what exactly do we mean by retirement planning?

Our retirement is a time in our lives when, having worked for a number of years, typically spanning decades, our employment comes to an end to make way for the next generation of workers and we, assuming we have planned for it effectively, enjoy the rest of our lives doing the things we love most with the people we love best.

The idea of planning for retirement, much like any other type of planning, involves:

- Establishing when you want to retire.
- Calculating how much you might need to retire on.
- Saving towards this target.

This isn't something you should be trying to figure out alone, by the way. When it's time, these questions should be tackled with the guidance of an expert like a financial adviser or retirement specialist, who are trained to help.

The focal point for all our retirement planning is our pension. This is a pot of money we save into over the course of our working lives, building it slowly and steadily in order to replace our salary when we stop working.

The best way to give our cash a fighting chance of growing enough in value to finance this time of our lives, is to invest our pension money across lots of different assets, building a pot that can last us until the end of our days.

But much like some of the other essential components of financial planning for our lives, for example budgeting, it's just not that exciting, is it?

I totally get it, of course. Why on Earth would you want to be planning for life after sixty when you haven't even decided what you want to do with your life in the first place? Seems like a whole lot of stress for little (immediate) gain. A headache you could do without thank you.

Or so you think. Because, in fact, retirement or pension planning, should be one of your top three financial goals at virtually every stage of your working life.
Here's why:

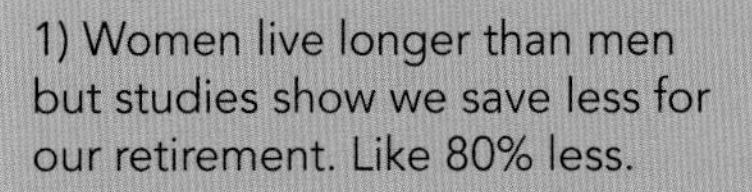

1) Women live longer than men but studies show we save less for our retirement. Like 80% less.

2) The realities of living longer mean that while we potentially enjoy the benefits of doing and seeing more in our lifetimes, as we age the likelihood of additional healthcare needs and associated costs increases. You may already have seen examples of this with some of your elderly loved ones.

3) Unfortunately, there is still evidence that women are often paid less than men, too, which means we need to work even harder to generate the cash to save adequately for our retirement in the first place.

It's impossible to sugar coat this situation so let's just say it exactly how it is...

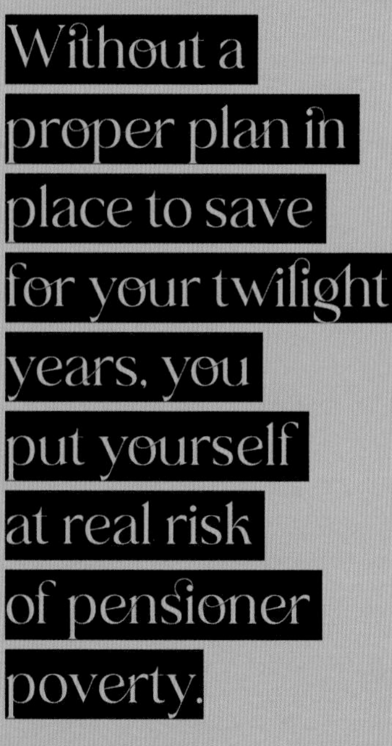

Or in other words, financial struggle and distress at a time in your life when you are well past your peak earning years.

Yet despite this, there is a big problem getting people to engage with their pensions properly. You may have heard some of these common reasons why:

"I'll never be able to save enough money to stop working and live comfortably so why bother?"

"I've left it too late for it to be worthwhile now."

"I need to live for today, who knows what will happen tomorrow."

But what if you could live for today AND secure yourself for tomorrow too? To eat a marshmallow now and have one in reserve for later?

That's when our Royal Money Mindset kicks in.

But first, we need to understand the practical steps to planning for retirement.

ACTIVITY

Have a conversation with the adults in your home about their retirement plans. What approach are they taking?

Different types of pension

Overall, there are two main types of pension you should know.

1) Workplace pension
2) Private pension

WORKPLACE PENSIONS

Depending on where you work, you may also be able to pay into a retirement savings plan through your employer as one of your employee benefits.

In some cases, any contributions you make will be matched or topped up by your employer to encourage you to save for later life. This could be a great way to accelerate your savings. So while it may be tempting to put it off and keep the cash in the short term, remember that any short term gains (that is the additional cash in your bank account) will almost certainly be outweighed by the long-term benefits of the investment returns you will generate over several decades (yes, seriously) of working.

Sure, the nights out and spontaneous weekends away are essential parts of your life too—so make sure you give them a place in your budget so you're not robbing Petra (future fabulous you) to pay Paula (current care-free you).

PRIVATE PENSION

But what about if you want to add an extra layer of protection to your pension planning outside of what you might receive through your employer?

Or maybe you're not eligible for a workplace plan because you're a freelancer or run your own business so are responsible for your own pension arrangements?

Then just as you might set up your own investment fund, you are also able to set up a personal private pension fund with more generous tax benefits to encourage you to save for later life yourself (ultimately reducing burden on the state system when you stop working).

The big question of course is when you intend to retire. The average age varies from country to country and you will have your personal preferences too. Being clear on this when you start your retirement savings and asking for help with calculating how much you need to save in order to retire at that age is a real boss move.

The other pension type worth mentioning, is a state or government pension.

SOCIAL SECURITY

As you probably already know, the role of government covers a number of different areas from education to the economy and countless others in between.

One of its biggest responsibilities, is to provide the infrastructure, funding, and resources to maintain the welfare of its citizens. It does this, in part, through the money it receives from taxation. There are a range of taxes that global citizens pay in their everyday lives, both across a variety of goods and services we pay for every day, as well as our earnings in the form of income tax and social security.

Social security, or the equivalent, is a monetary contribution made by workers in most countries around the world, to fund the welfare state. This may include but is not limited to, sick pay, and unemployment benefits and of course pensions. The purpose of this is to provide a lifeline to people when they need it most, either because they lack the financial resources to pay for these services themselves or, because having paid into the system all their working lives, as in the case of retired workers, they are now eligible to release some of the benefits.

Usually, our entitlement to these benefits in terms of how much we are able to access in cash terms is based on how much we pay into the system over the course of our working lives.

A bit like getting points on a loyalty card that you can redeem in future.

SO HOW DOES IT WORK?

Well, quite simply, as each new generation of workers pays into the system through deductions from their paycheck, their contributions are used to finance the latest set of pensioners who are about to begin retirement having themselves paid into the system for the set of pensioners before them.

The trouble, of course, is that it depends on getting the numbers just right. In practical terms this means...

1) That you have enough workers paying into the system at one end to finance those who need to benefit at the other end.

2) That you can predict, with a good degree of certainty, how long those people who are receiving social security will need to continue doing so.

It's one of the reasons we covered at the start of this chapter about why it's absolutely vital that young women in particular leave nothing to chance when it comes to saving for their retirement. Can you remember what this is?

If you said "because people are living longer" you'd be spot on.

And, as you now know, overall women all over the world live longer than men. A double whammy in our case.

So, what does this mean for our pension planning?

Well, let's put it this way, the smart money would be on hedging your bets, managing your risk, and not putting all your eggs in one basket. You know, a bit like our other investments.

Introducing FIRE

Ask most working adults, well into their careers, one of their top five daydreams when they get a spare moment. What would you expect to come up? Ask the adults in your life when they'd like to retire if money was no object. For most people, I think a desire to stop working ahead of traditional retirement age which has typically been when we reach our 60s, is top of the list. But for many, this remains a daydream.

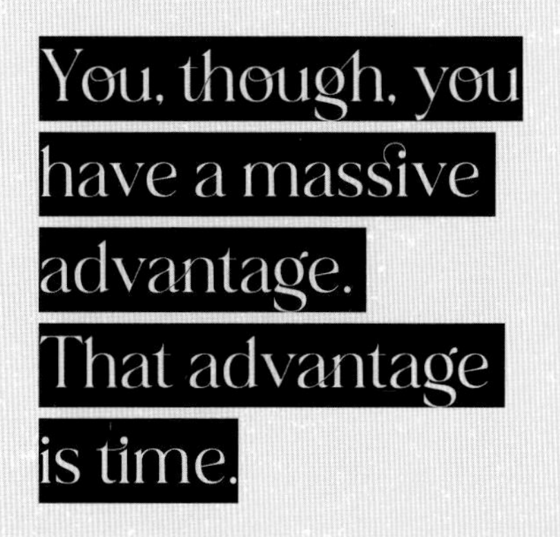

By thinking ahead and making savvy money moves now, you could potentially add yourself to the growing tribe of people joining the FIRE movement. **Financially Independent Retire Early**.

Some of the hallmarks of this approach include:

1) Saving up to 70% of your income through extreme budgeting and investing during your peak earning years (basically, when you're earning the most cash!) and then withdrawing a small percentage each year while the rest continues to be actively invested to replenish the money that's been taken. This is where your budgeting know-how will really come into its own.

2) Building a solid asset base in order to live on the profits. Examples include real estate as well as other investments.

3) Diversifying your income sources and generating passive income—for example, can you use your creative talents to generate cash without actively having to do a day job?

4) Living on less than your income—a key feature of FIRE converts is their resourcefulness. This may look different in different circumstances. It could mean stretching your cash as far as possible by living a frugal, minimalist lifestyle with few material possessions. Or it might include moving to those parts of the world where the standard of living is high and the cost of living is low. This works particularly well for the free-spirited FIRE devotee.

Just like any other type of pension planning, FIRE requires the discipline to save consistently and regularly for later life. The only difference here is that it is all done on speed and so requires careful consideration to decide whether it's right for you.

If this isn't an example of "go hard or go home" I don't know what is.

CROWN JEWELS

Your pension is in many ways the jewel in the crown of your investment portfolio. When we talked about taking a long-term view in investing, there's no better example than this.

Things to remember:

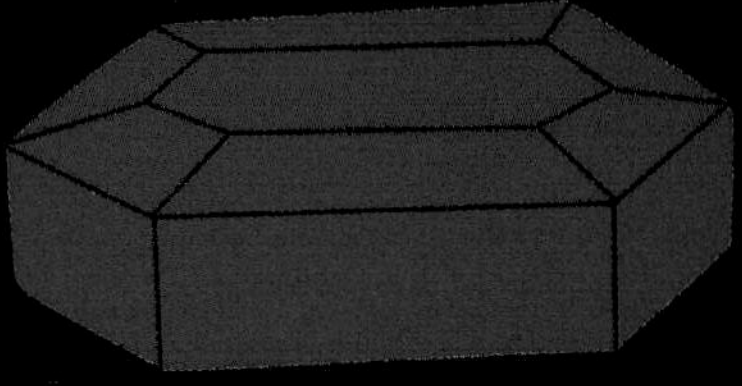

1.

Your pension is likely to be the longest-term investment you will have and is arguably one of the most important. Like your other investments, don't forget to check that your money is directed towards the right assets and is aligned to your retirement goals.

2.

Social security is unlikely to sustain you in future—make other arrangements.

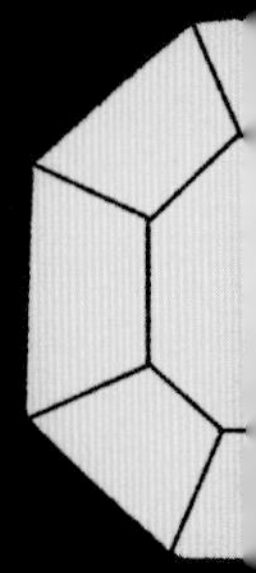

3.

Don't opt out of your workplace pension. It is the equivalent of turning down a monthly cash bonus.

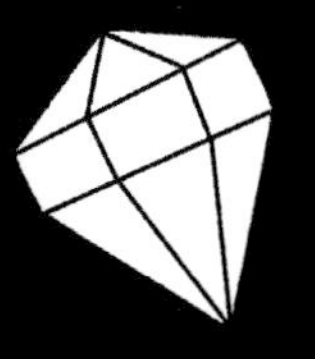

4.

As a rule of thumb... the longer you wait to start, the bigger your pension contributions will need to be to make up the shortfall.

5.

If earlier retirement is something that appeals to you, then the good news is time is on your side. Do your research on the FIRE movement and make a conscious decision based on the priorities you've set for your life.

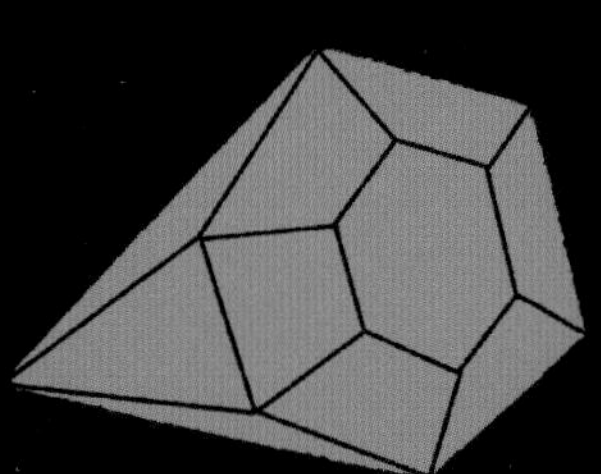

CHAPTER TWELVE

TEN LESSONS YOU SHOULD KNOW: A CHECKLIST

Hey you. Congratulations!

If you're reading this, you're now ten money lessons up on when you started. That's a big deal. Don't be afraid to shout about your newfound money knowledge to anyone who will listen. Chances are you'll be helping them too!

If you need a memory jogger of the main themes we've covered, here's a checklist. Go through and check you're happy with each lesson and if not revisit the relevant chapter. As many times as you like. This book is not intended to be a "one and done" type situation. Treat it as a handbook to be kept on standby at all times, ready for when you need a little money inspiration.

1) IMMEDIATE VS DEFERRED GRATIFICATION

Gratification is an important principle when it comes to how we spend or save our money. Understanding the different approaches and knowing when to switch between the two is your secret weapon.

2) IT'S NOT HOW MUCH YOU MAKE, BUT HOW MUCH YOU KEEP THAT COUNTS

BUDGETING IS A POWERFUL WAY TO INSTIL FINANCIAL SELF-DISCIPLINE AND ACHIEVE LONG-TERM FINANCIAL SUCCESS. IF YOU CAN'T MANAGE $10 YOU WON'T BE ABLE TO MANAGE A MILLION EITHER.

3) EARN YOUR OWN MONEY

There's no better money than money you've earned yourself. Here we discussed how to generate a little cash of your own as well as negotiating tactics you can practice for when you secure your first adult job.

4) INVESTING 101

Investing in different assets is a great way to help you grow your cash. Never overlook the importance of investing in your biggest asset by far—yourself.

5) YOU CONTROL YOUR MONEY, YOUR MONEY DOESN'T CONTROL YOU

CULTIVATING POSITIVE HABITS THAT WILL HELP YOU MAKE POWERFUL FINANCIAL DECISIONS ON AUTOPILOT IS A REAL BOSS MOVE.

6) CUT YOUR CLOTH ACCORDING TO YOUR SIZE

Live within your means and avoid debt!

7) THE FREEDOM FUND

DREAM BIG, PAINT IN THE DETAILS WITH YOUR IMAGINATION, THEN CALCULATE THE COST OF LIVING YOUR DREAMS AND DECIDE WHETHER OR NOT YOU'RE WILLING TO PAY THE PRICE.

8) YOUR MONEY TRIBE MATTERS

EVER HEARD THE EXPRESSION YOU'RE KNOWN BY THE COMPANY YOU KEEP? WELL, THIS APPLIES TO MONEY TOO. DO THE PEOPLE YOU SPEND THE MOST TIME WITH OUTSIDE YOUR FAMILY HAVE POSITIVE MONEY HABITS THAT RUB OFF ON YOU? IF NOT, CAN YOU HELP THEM LEVEL UP?

9) IF IT LOOKS TOO GOOD TO BE TRUE... IT PROBABLY IS

BEWARE "CASHFISHING" AND STAY VIGILANT TO FINANCIALLY ABUSIVE BEHAVIOR FROM OTHERS. DON'T BE AFRAID TO SPEAK TO SOMEONE YOU CAN TRUST TO ASK FOR HELP.

10) PLANNING FOR TOMORROW, TODAY

It may seem a long way off, but later-life planning is an important consideration that we should all make. The earlier you start, the lower the amounts you need to save each month. Plus you give yourself the best chance of joining the FIRE movement (financially independent, retire early) if that appeals to you.

CONTINUE THE CONVERSATION

Here are some ideas on what you can do now.

1) Lend this book to your friends or encourage them to buy their own.
2) Speak to your teacher about adding this to your school library.
3) Set up a book club date with your friends to discuss the lessons here and see whether they resonate with them too.
4) And finally, if you remember nothing from this book, here's one thing I'd like you to repeat to yourself if you're ever in doubt of your money-management skills...

CASH IS QUEEN
and so am I.

CASH IS QUEEN and so am I.

Glossary

50/30/20 method
An easy budgeting method that suggests you divide your monthly after-tax income into three spending categories: 50% for needs, 30% for wants, and 20% for savings and paying off debts.

Asset
A useful or valuable thing or person.

Automation
The creation and application of technology to monitor and control the production and delivery of products and services.

Bankruptcy
A legal process through which people or other entities who cannot repay debts to credits may seek relief from some or all of their debts.

Budget
A financial plan for a defined period of time.

Bureau of Labor Statistics (BLS)
The executive office of US statistics authority and is responsible for collecting and publishing statistics related to the economy, population, and society at national, regional, and local levels.

Buy Now Pay Later Scheme
A type of short-term financing that allows consumers to make purchases on credit and pay for them at a future date.

Cash saving
The amount of money left over after spending and other obligations are deducted from someone's income.

Cashfishing
A situation in which people having connected online, but never having met or seen one another face to face, might be tricked into sending, holding, and investing money.

Commodities
Basic goods used in the activity of buying and selling that is interchangeable with other goods of the same type.

Consumer Prices Index (CPI)
Measures the overall change in consumer prices over time based on a representative basket of goods and services.

Credit score
A number given to someone based on a variety of personal financial data and is used to determine whether the individual qualifies for a particular credit card, loan, mortgage, or service.

Credit union
A financial institution owned by its members as a mutual organization and offer banking and other financial-related services such as savings and mortgage lending.

Debt
A sum of money that is owed or due.

Deferred gratification
The idea that encourages individuals and groups to postpone immediate consumption or pleasure in the hope of gaining a more valuable or long-lasting reward in the long-run.

Delayed gratification
The resistance to the temptation of an immediate pleasure in the hope of obtaining a valuable and long-lasting reward in the long-run.

Digital native
Someone who has grown-up during the age of digital technology and is familiar with computers and the internet from an early age.

Diversification
The process of allocating capital in a way that reduces the exposure to any one particular asset or risk.

Earnings
Money gained from working or services.

Encrypted
Data that's been concealed by converting it into a code.

Entrepreneur
A person who sets up a business or

businesses, taking on financial risks in the hope of profit.

Envelope method
A method in which you take a few envelopes, write specific cash expense categories on each ones such as rent, shopping etc., and then put the money you plan to spend on those things into each envelope—usually done on a monthly basis.

Financial abuse
Involves someone using or misusing money, which limits and controls someone else's current and future actions and their freedom of choice.

Financial independence
The status of having enough income or wealth sufficient to pay one's living expenses for the rest of one's life without having to be employed or dependent on others.

Financial security
Having enough money to fund your lifestyle as well as work towards your financial goal.

Fixed
Predetermined and not able to change.

Forecast
To predict or estimate.

Freedom fund
Savings that you start building that can be used to aid in helping someone to live their dream life. It is completely separate to a rainy-day fund for emergencies.

Gender Pay Gap
The equality measure that shows the difference in average earnings between men and women. Women are generally considered to be paid less than men.

Gratification
Pleasure, satisfaction, or something that provides this source of pleasure.

Grooming
When someone builds a relationship, trust, and emotional connection with a child or young person so they can manipulate, exploit and abuse them.

Haphazard
Lacking any obvious principle of organization.

Immediate gratification
The experience of satisfaction or receipt of reward as soon as a response is made.

Income
Money received, especially on a regular basis, for work or through investments.

Index
An alphabetical list of names and subjects, with reference to the pages on which they are mentioned.

Inflation
A general increase in prices and fall in the purchasing value of money.

Interest
Money paid regularly at a particular rate for the use of money lent, or for delaying the repayment of a debt.

Investing
The act of allocating resources, usually money with the expectation of generating an income or profit.

Investment fund
A way of investing money alongside other investors in order to benefit from the advantage of working as part of a group.

Jargon
Special words or expressions used by a profession or group that is difficult for others to understand.

Liabilities
Something a person or company owes, usually a sum of money.

Market rate
The usual price of a product, service, or somebody's work per hour.

Mogul
An important or powerful person.

Money laundering
The process of making large amounts of money generated by a criminal activity appear to have come from a legitimate source.

Money script
Your unconscious

beliefs about money, often rooted in childhood, that affect your adult behaviors and perspectives.

Negotiating
A process that two or more parties go through to resolve an issue in a way that each party finds acceptable.

Non-fixed
Capable of change or movement.

Overdraft
Occurs when someone doesn't have enough money in their account to cover a transaction, but the bank pays for it anyway.

Passive income
A type of unearned income that is acquired automatically with minimal labor to earn or maintain it.

Penny-pinching
Unwilling to spend money.

Pension
A fund into which a sum of money is added during an employee's employment years and from which payments are drawn to support the person's retirement.

Pensioner poverty
Those who are of retirement age discover that they may not have enough pension to live on for the rest of their life.

Personal loan
Money borrowed from a bank, credit union, or online lender that you pay back in fixed monthly payments or instalments.

Retirement planning
Refers to financial strategies of saving, investments and distributing money meant to sustain oneself during retirement.

Return on Investment (ROI)
A metric used to understand the profitability of an investment.

Risk
The chance that an outcome or investment's actual gains will differ from an expected outcome or return.

Risk-reward trade-off
An investment principle that indicates that the higher the risk, the higher the potential reward.

Royal Money Mindset
To become confident with the handling of cash and money.

Savings account
A bank account that pays interest and is usually not able to be drawn on without notice or loss of interest.

Social security
Monetary assistance from the state for people with an inadequate or no income.

Stock market
Venues where buyers and sellers meet to exchange shares and other financial securities of public corporations.

Sustainable
When we are meeting our own needs without compromising the ability of future generations to meet their own needs.

Unconscious belief
Something we hold to be true but don't consciously think about.

Vision board
A collage of images and words representing a person's wishes or goals, intended to serve as inspiration or motivation.

Zero-sum method
A detailed budgeting method that suggests every part of your money has a role/place. All the money received monthly is split equally across the different activities that require spending.

Acknowledgements

DAVINIA

To call this book a labor of love would be a real understatement.

Massive thanks to the wonderful Ruth Cairns for her ingenuity and dedication, who was not only a cheerleader but a friend, and who spurred me on to keep trying even when things didn't always go according to plan.

To my editor Claire for her enthusiasm and encouragement and her compassion in the midst of setbacks during the writing process and for recognizing the importance of a book like this
for future generations of women.

My cheer squad led by my younger sister, Olivia, whose wisdom belies her years and who is one of few people who can pep talk me out of any meltdown, simply by reminding me who I am.

And of course, my constant source of inspiration, Sofia and Vivien. Being a mother of two daughters is the greatest privilege of my life and I hope this book will always serve as a reminder of just what you can accomplish with a little courage and a lot
of faith.

ANDREA

When we speak of money and investments and happiness, gratitude is also a good habit to adopt. Therefore I would like to thank Davinia for writing such an important book, and for her trust in me to illustrate her words. It's an honor to be a part of this project.

Thanks to Karissa as well, for putting our works together beautifully and guiding me when needed. I am very grateful for her patience and kindness. A big thank you to Claire, who offered me this opportunity. I am delighted to have been involved in this lovely project. My only regret is not having met you all to thank you in person.

I would also like to thank my parents, who provided me money education when this book didn't exist. And my partner Rod for his support throughout this project.

And finally, thanks to everyone who worked on the book and brought it to life.

For Sofia and Vivien and all budding rainmakers everywhere. — D.T.

First Published in 2023 by Frances Lincoln Children's Books,
an imprint of The Quarto Group.
100 Cummings Center, Suite 265D Beverly, MA 01915, USA.
T (978) 282-9590 F (978) 283-2742
www.quarto.com

A catalogue record for this book is available from the British Library.

ISBN 978-0-7112-7636-9

The illustrations were created digitally
Set in Mollie Gaston, Avenir

Published by Peter Marley
Designed by Karissa Santos
Edited by Claire Grace
Production by Dawn Cameron

Manufactured in Guangdong, China TT0822

9 8 7 6 5 4 3 2 1